DISCARDED

JUN 2 3 2025

ZK™

Ajax Without JavaScript™ Framework

HENRI CHEN AND ROBBIE CHENG

ZK™: Ajax Without JavaScript™ Framework

Copyright © 2007 by Potix Corporation

ISBN-13 (pbk): 978-1-59059-901-3

ISBN-10 (pbk): 1-59059-901-2

Printed and bound in the United States of America (POD)

Distributed to the book trade worldwide by Springer-Verlag New York, Inc., 233 Spring Street, 6th Floor, New York, NY 10013. Phone 1-800-SPRINGER, fax 201-348-4505, e-mail orders-ny@springer-sbm.com, or visit http://www.springeronline.com.

For information on translations, please contact Apress directly at 2855 Telegraph Avenue, Suite 600, Berkeley, CA 94705. Phone 510-549-5930, fax 510-549-5939, e-mail info@apress.com, or visit http://www.apress.com.

The source code for this book is available to readers at http://www.apress.com in the Source Code/Download section.

Contents

Part 1 ▪▪▪ Getting to Know the ZK Ajax Framework

Part 2 ▓▓▓ Applying Your ZK Knowledge

About the Authors

HENRI CHEN is the cofounder of the ZK Ajax Framework. He has more than 20 years' programming experience in various areas and programming languages. He has been writing Java programs since the initial release of the Java language in 1995 and ported JavaOS and HotJava to the world's first StrongARM-based network computer, which won the "Best of System" award in Comdex 1996. He is also an expert in thin-client programming, embedded systems, and Ajax web programming.

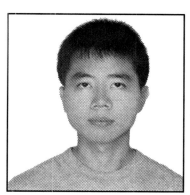

ROBBIE CHENG is an engineer on the ZK team. Though his major was English literature in college, he got his MBA degree in management of information systems. He has been an instructor in the use of the ZK Framework and the developer of zk registry, and has published many articles on the ZK web site. In addition to programming, his hobby is watching movies, and his favorite movie is *The Bridges of Madison County*.

About the Technical Reviewer

FRANK W. ZAMMETTI is a web architect specialist for a leading worldwide financial company by day and an active open source contributor by night. He is the author of two books—*Practical Ajax Projects with Java Technology* (Apress, 2006) and *Practical JavaScript, DOM Scripting, and Ajax Projects* (Apress, 2007)—and has another on the way. Frank has more than 13 years' of professional development experience under his belt (not to mention a few extra inches) and over 12 more (years, not inches!) of amateur experience before that. Frank lives in the United States with his wife, Traci, and his two kids, Andrew and Ashley. He is also visited nightly by beings from another world, which is fine, except that they won't stay off his grass no matter how nicely he asks, and you wouldn't believe how dry dark-matter-based impulse engines can make a lawn!

Introduction

In 1994, I developed an infrastructure, inspired by zApp and the Object Window Library (OWL), for developing an accounting system for Windows. In 2000, I developed another infrastructure, inspired by Struts and WebWorks, for developing another accounting system for the J2EE platform. After coaching and watching the development of both systems, I found that not only did the web edition require more advanced programming skills and prerequisites but its total cost was four times more than the client/server's. Worst of all, the user experience harkened back to the age of green terminals, though the look, after decorating with proper images and cascading style sheets, was modern and fresh.

I started wondering whether these problems were intrinsic to the web or if the programming model was simply inadequate. Looking back at the success of desktop applications in the 1990s, the event-driven, component-based programming model played a big role. Blessed by being easy to learn and develop, this model is the standard and best way to handle interactive and responsive user interfaces. Could this model be applied to web applications? After using ZK to develop several commercial projects, I believe I've got the answer—yes!

The reasoning behind that answer is what I want to share with you in this book. How can the ZK Framework make your life easy and your customers happy at the same time? How does ZK help you painlessly write a rich web application? How can you write a rich Ajax web application without learning JavaScript? How you can concentrate on improving your application itself rather than focusing on the plumbing required ensure browser compatibility? You will find your answers in this book.

This book is about how to make Ajax programming simple and easy—the core values of the ZK Framework—as simple as programming desktop applications and as easy as authoring HTML pages. Writing rich Ajax web applications can be very elaborate. On the browser side, you can program user interfaces with HTML, DOM, CSS, and JavaScript. On the server side, you can write business logic and data-access code with another language, such as Java. Then, you have to handle the browser-to-server messages with asynchronous HTTP. Finally, you still have to fight the incompatibility issues and JavaScript bugs across browsers.

This book will introduce you to painlessly programming Ajax applications with the ZK Framework. You are not required to write user interfaces on the browser side. Rather, you construct your applications on the server side with ZK's more than 160 Java components. The complex heterogeneous technologies involved in Ajax programming are automatically handled by ZK behind the scenes.

In this book, I tell you how to install and run ZK programs and how ZK completes its behind-the-scenes jobs, as well as explaining the important ZK components. I then walk you through creating a real web application, where you learn how to design the application screens, access the database, and write control code to coordinate the ZK presentation layer and the data accessing layer.

I sincerely hope this book helps you out of the old, painstaking, and time-consuming way of developing Ajax web applications. So read on to see how ZK makes your life easy and your customers happy at the same time. Enjoy your Ajax web programming experience.

Who This Book Is For

This book is especially for those who are interested in Ajax but don't want to learn to use JavaScript, CSS, and DOM, and who prefer not to deal with the incapability among browsers. To read this book, you should have basic knowledge of Java and HTML for building a web application with ZK.

How This Book Is Structured

This book is divided into two parts: the first part, "Getting to Know the ZK Ajax Framework" contains Chapters 1 through 4 and introduces you to the framework and the development environment setup:

- Chapter 1, "What Is the ZK Ajax Framework?" includes a basic introduction to ZK, which is a server-centric framework requiring little programming to use. Also, the architecture of ZK and how ZK realizes the idea of Ajax are explained.

- Chapter 2, "Getting Started with ZK," tells you how to set up the environment and to deploy the web application for running the ZK Framework.

- Chapter 3, "Building Your First ZK Application," demonstrates how to build the famous Hello World web application with ZK, along with providing some experience about how ZK components interact with each other.

- Chapter 4, "Introducing the Versatile ZK Components," introduces more concepts about using components and facilities provided by ZK to build a web application.

This book's second part, "Applying Your ZK Knowledge," explains how to build a real application with ZK:

- Chapter 5, "Setting Up the Development Environment," shows you how to set up Eclipse as the development environment.

- Chapter 6, "Creating a Real Web Application," provides a step-by-step explanation for using the ZK framework to implement the GUI of a ZK Pet Shop application, based on the famous Java Pet Store reference application.

- Chapter 7, "Linking the GUI to a Database," explores how to build the persistent layer with Hibernate and how the behind-the-scenes technology of ZK is implemented.

- Chapter 8, "Binding Data Automatically," introduces how to automatically move data between the GUI and controllers with ZK's data binding mechanism.

Downloading the Code

The source code for this book is available to readers at
`http://sourceforge.net/project/showfiles.php?group_id=156140` and at `http://www.apress.com` in the Source Code/Download section.

Contacting the Authors

You can contact Henri Chen at henrichen@zkoss.org and Robbie Cheng at robbiecheng@zkoss.org. Also, check out the ZK web site at http://www.zkoss.org.

■■■

PART 1

Getting to Know the ZK Ajax Framework

ZK is an open source Ajax web framework that enables a rich user interface for web applications with no JavaScript and little programming.

—ZK web site

In this part, we will discuss the various aspects of the ZK Ajax Framework and how Ajax is implemented without programming JavaScript.

CHAPTER 1

What Is the ZK Ajax Framework?

Over a decade, web applications have evolved from static HTML pages, to dynamic HTML (DHTML) pages, to pages using applets and Flash, and finally, to those incorporating Ajax (Asynchronous JavaScript and XML) technologies. Two great examples of Ajax are Google Maps and Google Suggest. Ajax breathes new life into web applications by delivering the same level of interactivity and responsiveness as desktop applications. However, unlike applets or Flash, Ajax is based on the standard browser and JavaScript, and no proprietary plug-in is required.

Ajax is a kind of next-generation DHTML; hence, it relies heavily on JavaScript to listen to events triggered by user activity and manipulates the visual representation of a page (that is, the document object model, or DOM) in the browser dynamically.

So, how can you easily incorporate Ajax into your web pages? Use the ZK Framework. Unlike most other Ajax frameworks, ZK does not require you to have any knowledge of JavaScript to develop Ajax-based web applications, since the ZK engine auto-generates the JavaScript code. To develop a web application with ZK, you need to know only a little about HTML. To simplify development of web application, the ZK team has also defined the ZK User Interface Markup Language (ZUML) to provide an intuitive way to create ZK components by simply declaring an enclosing tag, which is similar in format to an HTML tag.

Let's look at ZK's Live Demo web page to experience the magic of ZK (http://www.zkoss.org/zkdemo/userguide). This live demonstration explores various examples of ZK components that are built with Ajax and provides an online programming experience. You can modify the source code of each example online and see the results immediately.

Figure 1-1 shows demonstrations of two ZK components: Chart and Drag and Drop. Look at the Chart example shown on the left in Figure 1-1; the distribution of the pie chart will be updated automatically when you change the values of the programming categories. In the Drag and Drop component example, shown on the right in Figure 1-1, the sequence of each row will be reordered after dropping the dragged row onto the other one.

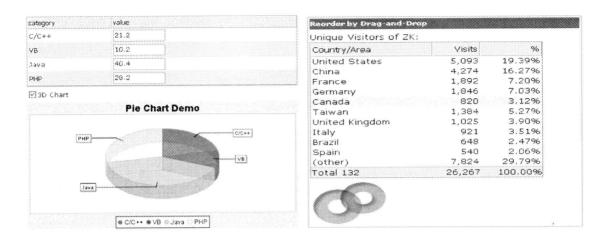

Figure 1-1. Live Demo shows how easily you can manipulate ZK components like these two.

ZK Ajax Framework

ZK is an event-driven, component-based framework to enable rich user interfaces for web applications. ZK includes an Ajax-based event-driven engine, a rich set of XML User Interface Language (XUL) and XHTML components, and a markup language called ZK User Interface Markup Language (ZUML).

With ZK, you represent your application in feature-rich XUL and XHTML components, and you manipulate them based on events triggered by user activity, as you have probably done for years in desktop applications. Unlike in most other frameworks, Ajax is a behind-the-scenes technology in ZK. ZK simplifies the development of rich Ajax web applications in the following ways:

- The event-driven engine brings the intuitive desktop programming model to web developers.

- The XUL and XHTML components enrich web applications by using off-the-shelf building blocks.

- The ZUML markup language makes the design of rich user interfaces as simple as authoring HTML pages.

In this chapter, I will explain how Ajax is accomplished by behind-the-scene mechanism of ZK. And, of course, the three most important characteristics of the ZK Framework will be introduced:

- It's a presentation layer tool.
- It's a server-centric framework.
- It's has a component-based GUI.

Ajax: Behind-the-Scenes Technology

The Ajax-based mechanism of ZK is realized by three important parts, as depicted in Figure 1-2: the ZK loader, ZK AU (asynchronous update) engine, and ZK client engine. The ZK loader and ZK AU engine are each composed of a set of Java servlets, and the ZK Client Engine is composed of JavaScript codes. Figure 1-2 illustrates the mechanism when the ZK loader receives a URL request at the first time.

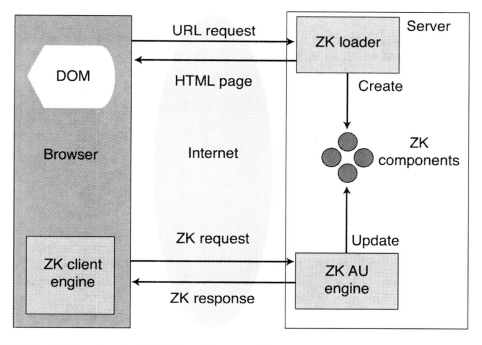

Figure 1-2. The ZK loader, the ZK AU engine, and the ZK client engine at work

The mechanism works like this:

1. The ZK Loader interprets an incoming URL request and generates a corresponding HTML page, including standard HTML, CSS, and JavaScript code, and ZK components at the server side.

2. The ZK loader sends the HTML page to the client and the ZK client engine. The ZK client engine resides on the client side for monitoring JavaScript events queued in the browser.

Note ➡ The ZK client engine is composed of a lot of JavaScript that is responsible for receiving events and updating the content of web pages.

---

3. If any JavaScript events are triggered, the ZK client engine will send those events (that is, those Ajax requests) back to ZK AU engine on the server side.

4. The ZK AU engine receives the Ajax requests, updates the properties of ZK components, and sends an Ajax response back to the client side.

5. The ZK client engine receives the response and updates the corresponding content in the browser's Document Object Model (DOM) tree.

This process is constantly repeated until the URL is no longer referenced by the user.

A Presentation Layer

ZK is designed to be as thin as possible, so it focuses only on the presentation tier. It does not require any other back-end technologies, and all of your favorite middleware, such as Java Database Connectivity (JDBC), Hibernate, Java Mail, Enterprise Java Beans (EJBs), and Java Message Service (JMS), works appropriately with ZK. Thus, you can build your web application with familiar technologies without learning new ones.

A Server-centric Event-Driven Framework

With most Ajax frameworks, the role of server is passive, since it is responsible only for providing and accepting data after receiving requests from the client side. The communication between components is quite complex and requires a lot of JavaScript programming, not to mention the problem of incompatibility among JavaScript and browsers.

By contrast, in ZK's solution, all the components are created on the server side, which makes communication between components easier since you can access these components directly on the server side. Moreover, the way components communicate with each other is event driven, which means interaction can be triggered by a user's activities on the client side or events sent from other components. In short, ZK mirrors the simplicity of developing desktop applications in the development of web applications and gives users more interactivity and more responsiveness.

A Component-Based GUI Toolkit

ZK is a component-based graphical user interface (GUI) toolkit. ZK provides more than 70 XUL-based and 80 XHTML-based components, and it provides the ZUML markup language for designing user interfaces. Programmers design their application pages in feature-rich XUL/XHTML components, which manipulate applications upon events triggered by the end user's activity. It is similar to the programming model found in desktop GUI-based applications.

Summary

Unlike other Ajax frameworks, which require a lot of knowledge about CSS, JavaScript, and DOM, ZK provides a shortcut for you to create Ajax-based web applications without learning other technologies, and developing ZK applications with ZUML requires you to know only a small amount about HTML. The ZK engine will handle the rest of the plumbing—generating HTML, CSS, and JavaScript code.

In addition, ZK makes it possible to develop web applications in an environment similar to desktop applications', since all components are also created on the server side. In other words, the relationship among components on the client side and components on server side is symmetric. Whenever you alter components running on the server, components on the client side are automatically updated in the browser by the ZK engine.

Furthermore, the behavior of UI components is triggered by user activities or events sent from other components, which makes it easy to understand the operation of your web application.

CHAPTER 2

Getting Started with ZK

ZK runs as a set of Java servlets inside a Java servlet container. In this chapter, I will guide you through the required installation step by step; it includes installing the Java runtime environment, installing a Java servlet container, and deploying the WAR file (I'm assuming that your operation system is Microsoft Windows 2000+).

Installing the Java Runtime Environment

The Java Runtime Environment (JRE) is necessary for running ZK and the Java servlet container (the web server used for ZK). If you have not installed any JRE, you should download one from the Sun web site (http://java.sun.com) and install it on your computer. I also suggest that you install the latest JRE version, at least version 5.0, since some Java servlet containers (such as Tomcat 5.5+) operate only under the JRE 5+ runtime environment. In addition, for the purpose of developing applications, it's best to install a Java Development Kit (JDK), which includes the JRE, a compiler, and a debugger. Install JDK 6.0 as follows:

1. Download the Windows online installation of JDK 6.0, Multi-language; it's the jdk-6-windows-i586-iftw.exe file at http://java.sun.com/javase/downloads/index.jsp.

2. After downloading the file, double-click the installer's icon. Then follow the instructions the installer provides to specify the location for installation.

Note ➡ For operating systems other than Windows, please refer to the online instructions at http://www.java.com/en/download/manual.jsp.

Installing the Java Servlet Container

The second step is to install a Java servlet container. I suggest you to install Apache Tomcat, which is one of the most popular servlet containers. Besides, it is pretty easy to install and use. In this example, we adopt Tomcat version 5.5.23

Using the Installer

You can install Tomcat 5.5.23 using the Windows Service Installer by following these steps:

1. Download the Windows Service Installer (apache-tomcat-5.5.23.exe) at http://tomcat.apache.org/download-55.cgi#5.5.23.

2. After downloading the file, double-click the icon to start the installation program, and follow the instructions on the screen to finish the installation. One thing you should remember to do is write down the HTTP port number (the default is 8080) of your configuration and the directory where the Tomcat is installed (we will call it $TOMCAT later). Also, remember the name and password of the administrator configured in your Tomcat installation, since you might need them for web application deployment.

Using the ZIP File

Alternatively, Tomcat provides a ZIP file for a quicker installation:

1. Download the ZIP file (apache-tomcat-5.5.23.zip) at http://tomcat.apache.org/download-55.cgi#5.5.23.

2. Unzip the file anywhere on your computer.

3. Set the JAVA_HOME variable as the base JDK installation directory.

4. From Start menu ➤ Control Panel ➤ System, click the Advanced tab. Then, click the Environment Variables button at the bottom; click the New button in the System Variable dialog; type the JAVA_HOME variable and value in the pop-up window; click OK to close the pop-up window; and click OK to close the program.

Deploying and Testing zkdemo-all.war

The last step is to download, from the ZK web site, the web application archive (WAR) file, zkdemo-all.war, which includes all necessary web-application-related files and Java archive (JAR) files, and then deploy it into your servlet container.

1. Download the latest version of the ZK demo file (zk-demo-x.x.x.zip) at http://www.zkoss.org/download/. The *x.x.x* represents the number of the latest stable version of ZK.

2. Unzip the file that you downloaded from ZK's web site, and find the file zkdemo-all.war.

3. Deploy zkdemo-all.war to Tomcat by copying the zkdemo-all.war file to the directory $TOMCAT/webapps/. Tomcat will handle the rest of work, including unzipping and deploying.

4. Activate the servlet container by clicking Start ➤ Programs ➤ Apache Tomcat 5.5 ➤ Monitor Tomcat. You should see an Apache icon on the Windows icon tray. Right-click the icon, and select Start Service. The red square on the icon turns green when Tomcat has been activated successfully.

5. To test the deployment, open your browser, and visit http://localhost:8080/zkdemo-all/userguide or http://localhost/zkdemo-all/userguide (the HTTP port can be omitted if your HTTP port is 80), and the port number should follow the configuration of your Tomcat. You should see ZK's Live Demo, the same one that's on ZK's web site.

Relative Libraries

The zkdemo-all.war file includes all necessary JAR files in the library directory within the WAR file, WEB-INF/lib. The following list introduces you to each JAR file and its function:

bsh.jar: BeanShell Java code interpreter

commons-el.jar: Apache implementation of Expression Language (EL) interpreter

commons-fileupload.jar: Apache implementation for uploading files commons-io.jar: Apache implementation for streaming I/O (used with file upload)

dojoz.jar: Dojo Ajax toolkit–related components

fckez.jar: FCKeditor HTML editor–related components

gmapsz.jar: Google Maps–related components

zcommon.jar: The common library for ZK

zhtml.jar: XHTML-related components

zk.jar: ZK kernel code

zkplus.jar: Acegi Security, Spring, Hibernate, and data binding integration codes

zul.jar: XUL-related components

zweb.jar: Web-related utility codes

Configuring web.xml

The web.xml file in the WEB-INF/ directory describes how a web application should be deployed. If you want to build your own ZK application, you have to properly set up the following configurations regarding servlets, listeners, and a filter in the file web.xml. Listing 2-1 shows an example web.xml:

Listing 2-1. The ZK web.xml *file*

```
<!-- ZK -->
<listener>
  <description>Used to clean up when a session is destroyed</description>
  <display-name>ZK Session Cleaner</display-name>
  <listener-class>org.zkoss.zk.ui.http.HttpSessionListener</listener-class>
</listener>

<servlet>
  <description>ZK loader for ZUML pages</description>
  <servlet-name>zkLoader</servlet-name>
  <servlet-class>org.zkoss.zk.ui.http.DHtmlLayoutServlet</servlet-class>
```

```
<!-- Must specify the URI of the update engine (DHtmlUpdateServlet).
It must be the same as <url-pattern> for the update engine.
-->
  <init-param>
    <param-name>update-uri</param-name>
    <param-value>/zkau</param-value>
  </init-param>
  <load-on-startup>1</load-on-startup>
</servlet>

<servlet-mapping>
  <servlet-name>zkLoader</servlet-name>
  <url-pattern>*.zul</url-pattern>
</servlet-mapping>

<servlet-mapping>
  <servlet-name>zkLoader</servlet-name>
  <url-pattern>*.zhtml</url-pattern>
</servlet-mapping>

<!-- Optional. For richlets. -->
<servlet-mapping>
  <servlet-name>zkLoader</servlet-name>
  <url-pattern>/zk/*</url-pattern>
</servlet-mapping>

<servlet>
  <description>The asynchronous update engine for ZK</description>
  <servlet-name>auEngine</servlet-name>
  <servlet-class>org.zkoss.zk.au.http.DHtmlUpdateServlet</servlet-class>
</servlet>
  <servlet-mapping>
    <servlet-name>auEngine</servlet-name>
    <url-pattern>/zkau/*</url-pattern>
  </servlet-mapping>
```

The preceding web.xml file includes configurations of a listener and two servlets for a running application of ZK. These two servlets include DHtmlLayoutServlet and DHtmlUpdateServlet. The DHTML layout servlet is zkLoader, and it's responsible for loading a ZUML page and creating components based on definitions of the page when the servlet container receives requests sent from the browser. The DHTML update servlet is auEngine; it is responsible for handling the ZK event request (which is an Ajax

XMLHttpRequest). I want to caution you that the update-uri URI of zkLoader must follow the url-pattern URL of auEngine, or your web application will not work properly.

In addition to building ZK web applications with ZMUL, developers can also use richlets to build web application with pure Java. A *richlet* is a small Java program that creates all the components necessary to respond to a user's request. However, richlets are designed especially for developers who have a deep understanding of ZK, since the developer has to decide how components should be constructed.

In addition, in order to distinguish pages created by richlets from those created with ZMUL, you need to define a new URL pattern for the ZK loader to hand over a user's request to the specified richlet. In the example in Listing 2-1, the ZK loader will hand over all requests under the URL of /zk/ to a richlet. Moreover, to specify the richlet to use for requests from a certain URL, you need to configure it in the zk.xml file. We'll look at how to do that in the next section.

Configuring zk.xml

In addition to web.xml, you might configure the zk.xml file for customized configuration of your ZK web application. Listing 2-2 demonstrates the configurations for a richlet for a web page's session timeout.

Listing 2-2. zk.xml *for ZK-specific configuration*

```
<!-- Optional -->
<!-- You can define any number of richlets as follows.
  Note: To use a richlet, you have to map zkLoader to /xx/* in web.xml,
  where xx could be any name. And the final URL will be /xx/richlet-url.
-->
<richlet>
  <richlet-class>org.zkoss.zkdemo.test.TestRichlet</richlet-class>
    <richlet-url>/test</richlet-url>
  <!-- Any number of initial parameters.
  <init-param>
    <param-name>any</param-name>
    <param-value>any</param-value>
  </init-param>
  -->
</richlet>

<!-- Optional -->
<session-config>
```

```
<!-- An empty URL can cause the browser to reload the same URL. -->
 <timeout-uri>/timeout.zul</timeout-uri>
</session-config>

<!-- Optional -->
<listener>
 <description>[Optional] Monitor the statistic</description>
 <listener-class>org.zkoss.zk.ui.util.Statistic</listener-class>
</listener>
```

Here are the important parts of the listing:

*   richlet must work together with the URL pattern (url-pattern) defined for the richlet in the web.xml file to determine which richlet class should handle requests from the specified URL pattern. In the example of zkdemo-all.war, for instance, requests for the URL http://localhost:8080/zkdemo-all/zk/test would be handled by the specified org.zkoss.zkdemo.test.TestRichlet class.

*   session-config defines the session attributes of a ZK web application. timout-uri is one of the child attributes that defines the response of a web page when a session times out. If the value is left blank, the browser will reload the same URL.

*   listener is used to configure an optional customized callback listener class, which requires the use of Java and thus should be implemented by developers. Here, the Java class Statistic is an example that is responsible for collecting statistics of page read/write operations.

Summary

The environment for running ZK web applications is pretty much the same as for running any other servlet application. To build your own ZK Live Demo, simply put the WAR file under the webapps/ directory in Tomcat, and the rest of work will be finished by Tomcat automatically.

Building your own ZK web application requires a little bit more effort—you need to set up the necessary configurations in web.xml and zk.xml. However, you can always just copy the web.xml and zk.xml files from zkdemo-all.war to your application and modify them. In fact, this is always how I start a new ZK web application project.

CHAPTER 3

Building Your First ZK Application

Since we set up the environment for running a ZK application in the previous chapter, in this chapter, I am going to guide you through making your first ZK application. We'll create the simplest, but most famous, program: Hello World. In addition, you will see how easy it is to customize a ZK component with its properties, as well as a demonstration of Ajax in ZK, and I'll explain its concept of behind-the-scenes technology. Now, follow the instructions in this chapter to complete your first mission!

Your First ZK Application: Hello World!

In this section, I'll explain how to build this application step by step.

1. First of all, create a file named myhello.zul in this directory: $TOMCAT/webapps/zkdemo-all/.

2. Use a text editor program or any kind of integrated development environment (IDE) to open this file.

Note ➡ Examples of IDEs you might use are Eclipse and NetBean. Instructions for installing Eclipse are included in Chapter 5.

---

3. Fill in this file with the content shown in Listing 3-1.

   Listing 3-1. myhello.zul

```
<window title="My First window" border="normal" width="200px">
Hello, World!
   </window>
```

4. Activate your Tomcat server.

5. Use a browser to visit http://localhost:8080/zkdemo-all/myhello.zul. Your screen should look like the one shown in Figure 3-1.

Note ➡ This URL depends on your configuration of Tomcat. Please refer to "Installing the Java Servlet Container" in Chapter 2 for more information.

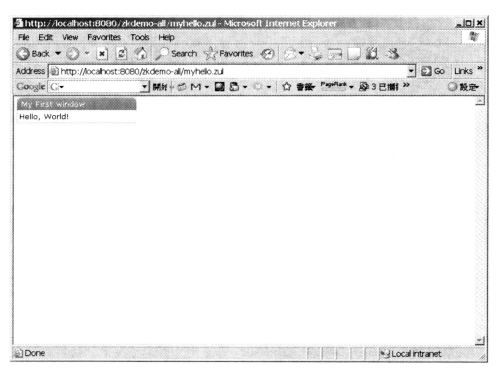

Figure 3-1. myhello.zul in Internet Explorer

The First ZK Component: Window

Congratulations! You have finished your first ZK application. The previous example introduced the first ZK component—window. Now, I am going to introduce you to how to customize the window component using its basic properties. Table 3-1 shows some of its properties.

Table 3-1. Properties of the Window Component

Property	Function	Value
title	Sets the title of the window	Any text
border	Sets the border style of the window	Normal or None (default is None)
height	Sets the height of the window	Number of pixels (e.g., 100px)
width	Sets the width of the window	Number of pixels (e.g., 100px)
closable	Sets whether or not this window can be closed	true or false
sizeable	Sets whether or not this window can be sized	true or false

Let's add some properties into our window component and see what happens. Start with the example in Listing 3-2 (to help you follow along with the example, the properties are in bold).

Listing 3-2. myhello.zul with More Properties

```
<window title="My Second window" border="normal" height="200px" ➡
width="200px" closable="true" sizable="true">
  Hello, World!
</window>
```

After editing myhello.zul, reload this page in your browser, and you should see the screen shown in Figure 3-2.

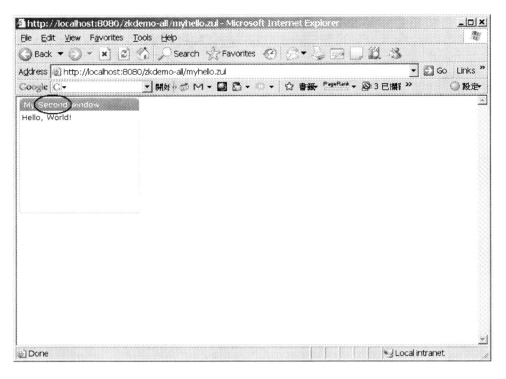

Figure 3-2. myhello.zul after modification

If you look at the title of the window, you should see that it has changed to "My Second window." You can now use your mouse to adjust the size of this window by clicking and dragging its lower right corner. The result is shown in Figure 3-3.

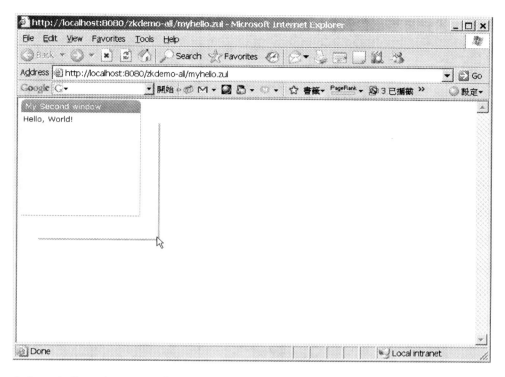

Figure 3-3. myhello.zul can now be resized.

Moreover, if you mouse over the upper right corner of this window, a square, white icon with a red *X* appears, as shown in Figure 3-4, and if you click the icon, the window will close.

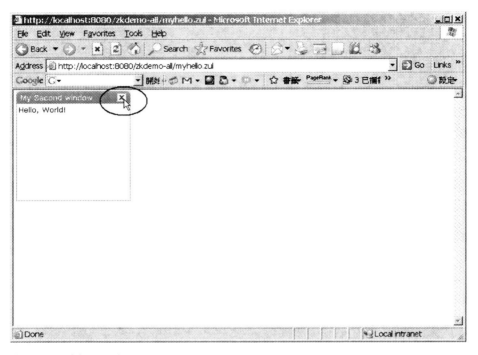

Figure 3-4. A closable window

But, you might argue, "This is not an Ajax application. There is no interactivity." Yes, at the moment, myhello.zul is just another JavaServer Page (JSP) page with special window component tags. So let's do some enhancement with Ajax.

Injecting Ajax to Your ZK Application

In this example, we are going to build a button in myhello.zul that will change the title of the window component if it is clicked. Please add the bold code in Listing 3-3 to myhello.zul.

Listing 3-3. myhello.zul with Ajax

```
<window id="win" title="My Second window" border="normal"
height="200px" width="200px" closable="true" sizable="true">
 Hello, World!
  <button label="change title"
  onClick="win.title=&quot;ZK applicaiton with Ajax&quot;"/>
</window>
```

Here's what you're doing with the new code:

1. Define an id for the window component.

2. Create a button by declaring a button component in myhello.zul.

3. Define a label component as a property of the button component, and type **="change title"** (with double quotes) following the label component.

Note ➡ A label component represents a piece of text. It can be created alone or attached to other components as a property.

---

4. Register an onClick event listener in the button component, which triggers an onClick event when this button is clicked.

5. Put the following line within double quotes in the onClick event listener to define the command when the onClick event is triggered:

```
win.title=&quot;ZK applicaiton with Ajax&quot;
```

This statement tells the ZK engine to change the title of the window component to "ZK application with Ajax" when the onClick event is triggered.

Note ➡ Since a .zul page is an XML page, you have to use " to escape the double quotes character (") so the XML parser can translate it correctly.

Reload myhello.zul in your browser, and the new button labeled "change title" should appear, as shown in Figure 3-5.

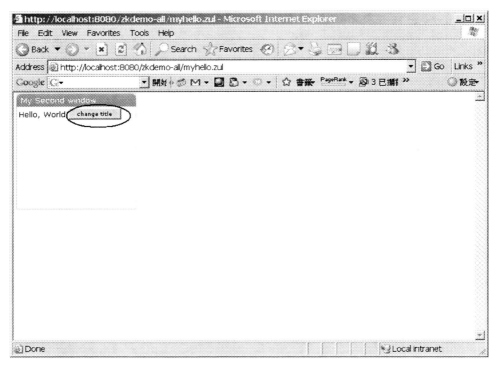

Figure 3-5. myhello.zul with an Ajax-driven button

If you click this button, the title of the window in the page will be changed to "ZK application with Ajax." The result is shown in Figure 3-6.

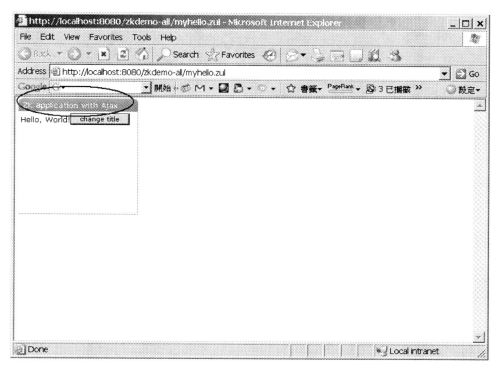

Figure 3-6. The title of the window has changed.

The behind-the-scenes workings of this example are illustrated in Figure 3-7.

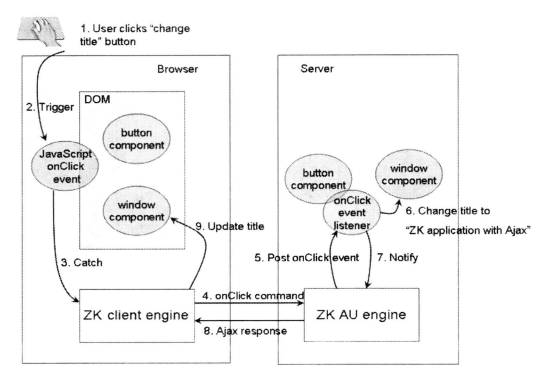

Figure 3-7. Flowchart of Ajax in ZK

Here's what's happening behind the scenes:

1. A user clicks the "change title" button.

2. A JavaScript onClick event is triggered.

3. The ZK client engine catches this event.

4. ZK client engine sends the onClick command back to the server via an Ajax XMLHttpRequest.

5. ZK AU engine on the server side receives the command sent by the ZK client engine and sends an onClick event to the server-side onClick event listener registered in the button component.

6. The onClick event listener updates the title of window component on the server side to "ZK application with Ajax".

7. The onClick event listener notifies the AU engine that its execution has finished.

8. The ZK AU engine wraps the update command into the proper Ajax response and sends them back to browser via an XMLHttpResponse.

9. The ZK client engine receives the response from the browser and updates the DOM tree accordingly.

In short, the ZK AU engine and the ZK client engine work together as pitcher and catcher. They deliver events happening in the browser to the application running at the server and update the DOM tree at the browser based on how components are manipulated by the application.

Summary

After reading the step-by-step guidelines in this chapter, you should be able to develop a simple ZK application. This chapter's example demonstrates two important characteristics of ZK: it's component-based and event-driven.

Developing ZK applications with ZUML can save time, since you can easily determine the purposes of ZK component from their names. Using ZUML, you can change the look or behavior of components by simply adding or editing their properties.

This chapter also provided a simple example with Ajax technology in which the title of a window in a web page is changed when the user clicks the button within that window. The behind-the-scenes technology is handled by the ZK client and AU engines, and no JavaScript knowledge is required to write the Ajax application.

In the next chapter, I will introduce more ZK components to you, and of course, you'll get to practice more with Ajax.

.

CHAPTER 4

Introducing the Versatile ZK Components

After reading through the previous chapters, you should have some feeling about how to write ZK web applications. In this chapter, I will discuss the basic concepts of the ZK Ajax Framework in more detail, which will prepare you to create the real application in Part 2 of this book.

Components, Pages, and Desktops

A *component* is a user interface (UI) object, such as a label, a button, or a tree. It defines the visual representation and behaviors of a particular user interface *element*. By modifying the component itself or manipulating the component structure, you can control to the visual representation of an application in the client. All ZK component implements the org.zkoss.zk.ui.Component interface.

A *page* is a collection of components. Pages are members of the org.zkoss.zk.ui.Page class, and they contain components that will be displayed in certain portions of the browser. A page is automatically created when the ZK loader interprets a ZUML page. As a ZK application interacts with user, components might be added to a page, and some might be removed from the page.

A desktop (of class org.zkoss.zk.ui.Desktop) is a collection of pages for serving the same URL request. As a ZK application interacts with user, pages might be added to a desktop, and some might be removed from a desktop.

Note ➡ A component is of two worlds. Besides being a Java object on the server, a component has a visual part in the browser when it belongs to a page. That is, when a component is attached to a page, its visual part is created in the browser. When a component is detached from a page, its visual part is removed.

The Component Life Cycle

ZK framework assumes some processing sequences regarding loading and updating pages that might affect how you write the ZK applications. In this section, we'll look at the life cycle of ZK components so that you have a better understanding of the mechanism of ZK framework.

The Life Cycle of a ZUML Page

It takes four phases for a ZK loader to load and interpret a ZUML page:

1. Page initialization

2. Component creation

3. Event processing

4. Rendering

The Page Initialization Phase

In this phase, ZK runs the processing instructions, called init. If no such processing instructions are defined, this phase is skipped.

For each init processing instruction with a class attribute, an instance of the specified class is constructed and its doInit() method is called, for example, <?init class="MyInit"?> specifies MyInit class as an initiator of the page. What the class will do, of course, depends on your application requirements.

Another way to pass the init processing instruction is to specify a zscript file, for example, <?init zscript="/my/init.zs"?>. Then, the zscript file will be interpreted at the Page Initial phase.

Note ➡ The page is not yet attached to the desktop when the page initialization phase executes.

The Component Creation Phase

In the component creation phase, the ZK loader interprets a ZUML page; it creates and initializes components according to the specifications in the page. The several steps in this phase are as follows:

1. For each element, the ZK loader examines the if and unless attributes to decide whether they are true. If not, the element and all of its child elements are ignored.

2. If the forEach attribute is specified with a collection of items, ZK performs steps 3–7 for each item in the collection.

3. The ZK loader creates a component based on the element name or the class specified in the use attribute, if any.

4. The members of the component's class are initialized one by one in the order that attributes are specified in the ZUML page.

5. The ZK loader interprets any nested elements and repeats the whole procedure.

6. The loader invokes the afterCompose() method if the component implements the org.zkoss.zk.ui.ext.AfterCompose interface.

7. After all children are created, the onCreate event is sent to this component, so that the application can initialize the content of additional elements later. The onCreate events are posted for child components first.

The Event Processing Phase

In the event processing phase, ZK invokes each listener for each event queued for the desktop one by one. An independent thread is started to invoke each listener, so it can be suspended without affecting the processing of other events.

Note ➡ During processing, an event listener might fire other events.

The Rendering Phase

After all events are processed, ZK renders the components into a regular HTML page and sends this page to the browser. To render a component, the redraw() method is called.

Note ➡ The redraw() method will not alter any content of the component.

Updating Pages

It takes three phases for the ZK AU engine to process ZK requests sent from clients:

1. Request processing

2. Event processing

3. Rendering

   ZK AU Engine pipelines ZK requests into queues; it creates one queue per desktop. Therefore, requests for the same desktop are processed sequentially. Requests for different desktops are processed in parallel.

The Request Processing Phase

Depending on the specifications in the request, the ZK AU engine might update the content of affected components so that their content is the same as what is shown on the client. Then, it posts corresponding events to the queue.

The Event Processing Phase

This phase is the same as the event processing phase of loading a ZUML page. It processes events one by one and uses an independent thread for each.

The Rendering Phase

After all events are processed, ZK renders the updated components, generates corresponding ZK responses, and sends these responses back to the client. Then, the client engine updates the DOM tree at the browser based on the responses.

Whether you're redrawing the whole visual representation of a component or updating an attribute at the browser depends on the implementation of components. As the component developer, it's up to you to balance interactivity and simplicity in deciding whether to update or redraw.

Component Garbage Collection

Unlike many component-based GUIs, ZK has no destroy() or close() method for components. Like in the World Wide Web Consortium (W3C) DOM specification, a component is removed from the browser as soon as it is detached from the page. It is shown as soon as it is attached to the page.

More precisely, once a component is detached from a page, it is no longer managed by ZK if the application does not keep any reference to it. The memory occupied by the component will be released by the Java Virtual Machine (JVM) garbage collector. However, if the application holds a reference to the component, it will not be collected with the garbage.

Using Component Attributes

In the following section, I will introduce you commonly used attributes of component in ZUML pages. One of the crucial attributes is id, which assigns a identifier to a component. You can decide whether to create a component or not by specifying the statement in if or unless attributes. And, you can determine how many components will be created using the forEach attribute. Moreover, you can replace the default Java class of a component by assigning another Java class with the use attribute.

The id Attribute

To reference a component in Java code or EL expressions, you should assign an identifier to it using an id attribute. In Listing 4-1, an identifier "label" is assigned for label so that the ZK engine can identify this label component at the server for manipulating its value.

Listing 4-1. An id Attribute Example in Java

```
<window title="Vote" border="normal">
  Do you like ZK?
  <label id="label"/>
  <separator/>
  <button label="Yes" onClick="label.value = self.label"/>
  <button label="No" onClick="label.value = self.label"/>
</window>
```

The code within the double quotes of the onClick event listener will be sent back to the server and interpreted as Java code. In this statement, self is an implicit object referring to the button component itself, and label references the label component.

If you click the Yes button on the screen, the word "Yes" should appear in answer to the question "Do you like ZK?" See Figure 4-1. If you click the No button, the word "Yes" will be replaced with "No."

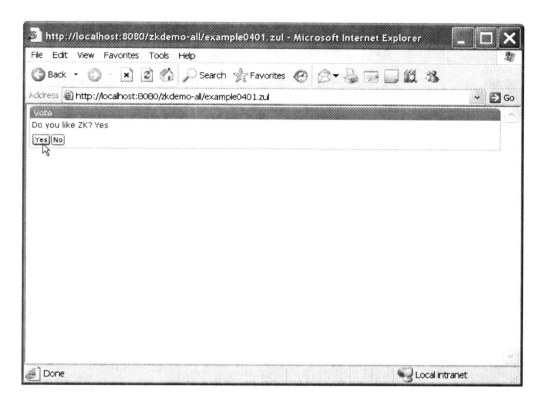

Figure 4-1. Using an id attribute in Java

Listing 4-2 is another example for referencing a component, this time in an EL expression. The string to use for the label (that is, the value of label) is taken from the source text box (the value of textbox with the id of "source"). First of all, declare a textbox component whose id is "source". Next, set the value of the label component equal to the value of textbox by using an EL expression to identify the textbox component.

Listing 4-2. An id Reference Example with an EL Expression

```
<window>
  <textbox id="source" value="ABC"/>
  <label value="${source.value}"/>
</window>
```

Save this example file under $TOMCAT/webapps/zkdemo-all/, and open a browser to visit the page; you should see the screen shown in Figure 4-2.

Two "ABC" strings appear, one in an input field and the other outside this field. If you want to change the string shown on the screen, you could edit the value of textbox in the ZUML page and reload it.

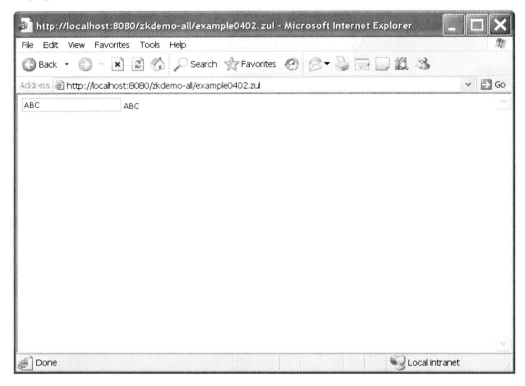

Figure 4-2. An id attribute example using an EL expression

The if and unless Attributes

The if and unless attributes are used to define a true-false statement for determining whether to create a component or not. In example shown in Listing 4-3, an EL expression is used to determine whether the parameter vote is true or false. These two labels will be created if the value of vote is true; otherwise, neither of them will be created. If both of these attributes are specified, the component won't be created unless they are both true.

Listing 4-3.An if and unless Example

```
<window>
  <label value="Vote 1" if="${param.vote}"/>
  <label value="Vote 2" unless="${!param.vote}"/>
</window>
```

Figure 4-3 shows the result when you visit this page with a vote parameter whose value is true, but you could try to visit this page with different value of vote, for example, false, null, none, and so on to see what will happen to these components.

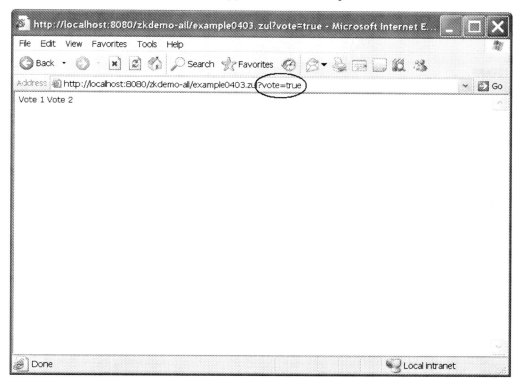

Figure 4-3. The if and unless example

The forEach Attribute

The forEach attribute is used to determine how many components will be created. If you specify a collection of objects to this attribute, the ZK loader will create a component for each item in the specified collection. For example, in the following ZUML page, we declare an array, contacts, within a special <zscript> tag in which you can write Java code. The listitem element will be evaluated three times, and three listitem components ("Monday", "Tuesday", and "Wednesday") will be generated.

Listing 4-4. forEach Attribute Example

```
<window>
  <zscript>
    contacts = new String[] {"Monday", "Tuesday", "Wednesday"};
  </zscript>
  <listbox width="100px">
    <listitem label="${each}" forEach="${contacts}"/>
  </listbox>
</window>
```

When evaluating an element with the forEach attribute, objects from the collection (contacts in the previous example) are assigned the each variable one by one. Thus, the previous ZUML page is the same as the following lines:

```
<listbox width="100px">
  <listitem label="Monday"/>
  <listitem label="Tuesday"/>
  <listitem label="Wednesday"/>
</listbox>
```

The use Attribute

Embedding code improperly in pages might cause a maintenance headache, so it's best to separate control code from the code for the UI. There are two ways to separate code from views.

First, you could put these control codes in a separate Java class, and then register event listeners to invoke the proper methods accordingly. For example, you could invoke your methods to initialize or to cancel a process by registering the onCreate(), onOK(), and onCancel() event listeners to invoke those methods defined in MyClass class:

```
<window id="main" onCreate="MyClass.init(main)"
  onOK="MyClass.save(main)" onCancel="MyClass.cancel(main)"/>
```

For this to work, you must have a Java class called MyClass as shown in Listing 4-5.

Listing 4-5. MyClass.java

```
import org.zkoss.zul.Window;
public class MyClass {
  public static void init(Window main) {
   //does initialization
  }
  public static void save(Window main) {
   //saves the result
  }
  public static void cancel(Window main) {
   //cancel any changes
  }
}
```

The other option for separating the view code is to assign the use attribute to specify a class to replace the default component class:

```
<window use="MyWindow"/>
```

In this case, you must have a Java class called MyWindow, as shown in Listing 4-6.

Listing 4-6. MyWindow.java

```
import org.zkoss.zul.Window;
public class MyWindow extends Window {
  public void onCreate() {
   //does initialization
  }
  public void onOK() {
   //save the result
  }
  public void onCancel() {
   //cancel any changes
  }
}
```

ID Spaces

As mentioned previously, ZK allows you to reference each component by its id attribute. However, a visual representation is usually decomposed into several ZUML pages; for example, you might have a page for a purchase order and a modal dialog page for the payment terms. If all components are uniquely identifiable in the same desktop, you have to maintain the uniqueness of all identifiers for pages that might be created for that same desktop, which often results in the problem of identifier conflict. ZK has introduced the concept of ID space to deal with this issue.

An *ID space* is composed of a *space owner and its fellow components. The space owner is like a file folder, and the fellow components like files within it. In a file system, files with the same name can coexist if they are put in different file folders. In the same way, you can assign the same ZUML identifier for components if they reside in different ID spaces. In other words, the uniqueness of component identifiers is guaranteed only within the scope of a single ID space.

Note ➡ A component that implements the org.zkoss.zk.ui.IdSpace interface denotes that itself and all of its descendant form an independent ID space.

In addition to resolving the problem of identifier conflict, ID spaces make it easy to refer to a component inside or outside of an ID space by simply invoking the getFellow() method.

Getting a Fellow that's Inside the ID Space

Components within the same ID space can refer to each other by invoking the getFellow(componentID) method. In addition, there are two ways to retrieve the space owner. One is by invoking the getSpaceOwner() method of fellow components, and the other is by invoking the getFellow(spaceOwnerID) method, since the space owner is also a fellow component of this ID space. As a result, there is no hierarchical relationship between the space owner and its fellow components; the space owner is just an identifier in an ID space, like a name of file folder.

Getting a Component that's Outside the ID Space

It is easy to retrieve any component within another ID space by invoking the getFellow(spaceOwnerID, componentID) method, which is much the same as getting a file in a file folder.

Listing 4-7 provides an example illustrating this idea. The window component is a typical space owner. In this example, there must be at least two ID spaces, since there are two window components in this page. Both of these ID spaces include a label component, and you could have the same identifier labelD for each of these two label components (since they are in different ID spaces). As a result, the problem of identifier conflict is resolved by using ID spaces to divide a ZUML page into a number of zones, like folders.

A hierarchical relationship does exist between space owners. A space owner could be a fellow component of another ID space when a space owner is embedded within another ID space. In this example, the "winC" component is a fellow component of "winA" since it is embedded within the ID space of the "winA" component. Therefore, if you want to retrieve a component within the ID space of "winC", for example, labelD, you should invoke the getFellow() method in the following format:

getFellow("winC").getFellow("labelD")

Listing 4-7. An ID space example

```
<?page id="page1"?>
<zk>
  <window id="winA">
    <label id="labelB" value="Label B"/>
    <window id="winC">
      <label id="labelB" value="Label B"/>
    </window>
  </window>
  <vbox id="vboxD">
   <label id="labelE" value="Label E"/>
  </vbox>
</zk>
```

In addition, the page component is another space owner in this example. In this ID space, page is the space owner, and winA, *vboxE, and *labelF are its fellow components. The relationship among these components is illustrated in Figure 4-4.

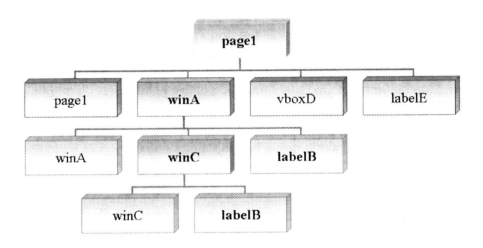

Figure 4-4. The relationship among components

Note ➡ Neither vbox nor label implements the org.zkoss.zk.ui.IdSpace interface; as a result, they are fellow components of the ID space (page1).

In Listing 4-7, there are, in fact, a total of three ID spaces—two window components, winA and winC, and a page component, page1, which is another kind of space owner:

- The page1 ID space has winA, vboxF, and labelG as fellows.

- The winA ID space has winA, hboxB, labelD, winC, labelE as fellows.

- The winC ID space has winC and labelE as fellows.

To make referencing components easier, ZK also provides a Path utility class with which you can access any component within any ID space with an ID space directory format, just like accessing a file within a file system directory. For example, if you want to get the labelD component of this page, you can call Path.getComponent("/winA/labelD"). If you want to get labelE, you can call Path.getComponent("/winA/winC/labelE"). Here, the root slash (/) means the current page.

Getting a Component from Another Page

Listing 4-8 builds page2.zul, which includes page1.zul. Then, page1 and page2 form a desktop.

Listing 4-8. Creating Two Pages on One Desktop

```
<?page id="page2"?>
<window id="winH">
  <label id="labelI" value="Label I"/>
  <include src="page1.zul"/>
</window>
```

To reference a cross-page component, you have to go through the desktop. For example, to reference labelD of page1 from labelI of page2, you could call this method:

labelI.getDesktop().getPage("page1").getFellow("winA").getFellow("labelD")

You could also use the Path utility to perform a cross-page reference:

Path.getComponent("//page1/winA/labelD")

Here the double slash (//) means the current desktop.

Using zscript and EL expressions

Though you've learned how to separate control code from the view, ZK provides a way to declare variables or methods within the ZUML page directly when necessary using the zscript element. Besides, ZK also supports EL expressions for accessing variables defined within zscript element. Their uses are introduced in the following paragraphs.

zscript

The zscript element, shown in Listing 4-9, is a special ZUML element to define Java code to be evaluated when a ZUML page is rendered. It is most often used to initialize page or component creation or to declare global functions.

Listing 4-9. zscript Example

```
<window id="winHello" title="Hello" border="normal">
 <button label="Say Hello" onClick="sayHello()"/>
 <zscript>
  int count = 1;
    void sayHello() {
//declare a global function
    alert("Hello World! "+ count++);
  }
 </zscript>
</window>
```

Every time you press the Say Hello button, the onClick event handler's sayHello()method, which is defined globally in zscript, is called, and the variable count is increased. Figure 4-5 shows the result after the button has been clicked three times.

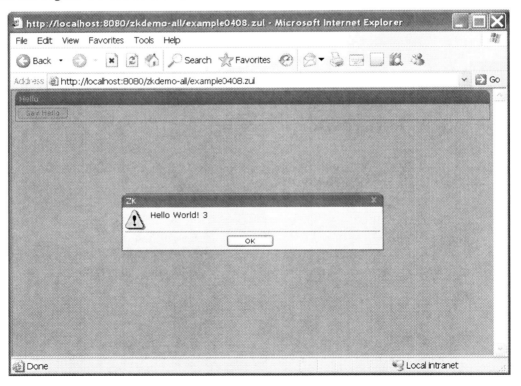

Figure 4-5. The zscript example after clicking the Say Hello button three times

If you prefer to separate code from views, you could put the Java code in a separate file, like sayHello.zs as shown in Listing 4-10. Then, you use the src attribute of the zscript to reference it, as shown in Listing 4-11.

Listing 4-10. sayHello.zs Used in Listing 4-11.

```
  int count = 1;
void sayHello() { //declare a global function
alert("Hello World! "+ count++);
}
```

Listing 4-11. A zscript Example using the src Attribute

```
<window title="Hello" border="normal">
  <button label="Say Hello" onClick="sayHello()"/>
   <zscript src="sayHello.zs"/>
</window>
```

EL Expressions

Just like you can in JSP pages, you can use EL expressions in any part of ZUML pages, except within the names of attributes, elements, and processing instructions. ZUML EL expressions use the same syntax as JSP EL expressions, that is, ${expr}. See Listing 4-12 for an example.

Listing 4-12. EL Expression Example

```
<window title="EL Test" width="200px">
<zscript>
   String abc = "ABC";
</zscript>
  <button label="${abc}"/>
</window>
```

When an EL expression is used as an attribute value, it can return any kind of object as long as the component accepts that object as input. For example, the following expression will be evaluated as a Boolean object: <window if="${some > 10}">

Events

An event is of the class org.zkoss.zk.ui.event.Event and is used to notify an application what has happened. Each type of event is represented by a distinct class. For example, org.zkoss.zk.ui.event.MouseEvent denotes a mouse activity, such as clicking.

To respond to an event, an application must register one or more event listeners to the event. There are three ways to register an event listener to a component. One is by specifying the onXxx event listener as the component's attribute, where Xxx represents the name of the action, as shown in Listing 4-13.

Listing 4-13. Event Handler as a Defined Attribute

```
<window title="Hello" border="normal">
  <button label="Say Hello" onClick="alert(&quot;Hello World!&quot;)"/>
</window>
```

In Listing 4-13, onClick is the event that fires to the button object. The event handling code for the onClick event is alert("Hello World!").

The second way to register an event listener is by defining the onXxx() method in the associated component's class; see Listing 4-14.

Listing 4-14. An Event Handler as a Defined Method

```
<window title="Hello" border="normal">
  <zscript>
    class MyButton extends Button {
      public void onClick(MouseEvent event) {
        Messagebox.show("Hello World!");
      }
    }
  </zscript>
  <button label="Say Hello" use="MyButton"/>
</window>
```

Calling the addEventListener() method for the component or the page you want to listen, as shown in Listing 4-15, is the last way to register an event listener.

Listing 4-15. An Event Handler as a New Event Listener

```
<window title="Hello" border="normal">
  <button id="hellobtn" label="Say Hello"/>
  <zscript>
```

```
hellobtn.addEventListener("onClick", new EventListener() {
  public void onEvent(Event event) {
    Messagebox.show("Hello World!");
  }
});
</zscript>
</window>
```

In addition to events triggered by user activity in the browser, an application can fire events by using the sendEvent() and postEvent() methods from the org.zkoss.zk.ui.event.Events class, for example, Events.postEvent(new Event(. . .)).

ZUML and XML Namespaces

Recall that ZUML is an XML-based language used to describe the visual representation of a page. ZUML divides off the dependency of the set of components to use. In other words, different types of components, such as XUL and XHTML, can be used simultaneously in the same ZUML page, and other markup languages can be added transparently. However, if two or more types of components are used in the same page; you have to use XML namespaces to distinguish them. Listing 4-16 shows an example of mixing two types of components.

Listing 4-16. Mixing ZUL and ZHTML Components

```
<window title="mix HTML demo"
 xmlns:h="http://www.w3.org/1999/xhtml"
 xmlns:x="http://www.zkoss.org/2005/zul"
 xmlns:zk="http://www.zkoss.org/2005/zk">
 <h:table border="1">
  <h:tr>
   <h:td>
    column 1
   </h:td>
   <h:td>
    <listbox id="list" mold="select">
     <listitem label="AA"/>
     <listitem label="BB"/>
    </listbox>
   </h:td>
   <h:td>
    <h:ul id="ul">
```

```
      <h:li>The first item.</h:li>
      <h:li>The second item.</h:li>
    </h:ul>
    <h:input type="button" value="ZHTML button Add Item"
      zk:onClick="addItem()"/>
    <x:button label="ZUL button Add Item" onClick="addItem()"/>
    <zscript>
      import org.zkoss.zhtml.Li;
      import org.zkoss.zhtml.Text;
      void addItem() {
        Li li = new Li();
        li.setParent(ul);
        new Text("Item "+ul.getChildren().size()).setParent(li);
      }
    </zscript>
    </h:td>
  </h:tr>
 </h:table>
</window>
```

Creating a Real Modal Dialog

ZK supports real modal dialogs; the application's event thread processing is suspended and waits for a user's action to resume. This feature tremendously simplifies web programming in ZK. To further simplify some common tasks, ZK supports the commonly used message box and file upload dialogs.

Messagebox

Messagebox (that is, org.zkoss.zul.Messagebox) is a utility class to show message boxes. It is typically used to alert a user when an error occurs or to prompt a user for a decision. An example is shown in Listing 4-17.

Listing 4-17. Example of Messagebox

```
if (Messagebox.show("Remove this file?",
  "Remove?", Messagebox.YES | Messagebox.NO,
  Messagebox.QUESTION) == Messagebox.YES) {
    ...//remove the file
}
```

Since it is common to alert a user of an error, a global function called alert() is available for zscript. The alert() function is a shortcut of the show() method in the Messagebox class. For example, the following two statements are equivalent:

alert("Wrong");

Messagebox.show("Wrong");

Fileupload

The Fileupload (org.zkoss.zul.Fileupload) utility class prompts a user for uploading a file from the browser. The get method will show a dialog automatically that prompts the user at the browser for specifying a file for uploading. It won't return until the user has uploaded a file or clicked the cancel button. The example code is demonstrated in Listing 4-18.

Listing 4-18. Example of Fileupload

```
<window title="Fileupload Demo" border="normal">
 <image id="image"/>
 <button label="Upload">
  <attribute name="onClick">{
   Object media = Fileupload.get(); //the upload dialog appear
   if (media instanceof org.zkoss.image.Image)
     image.setContent(media);
   else if (media != null)
     Messagebox.show("Not an image: "+media,
       "Error", Messagebox.OK, Messagebox.ERROR);
  }</attribute>
 </button>
</window>
```

Implementing Macro Components

ZK supports implementing a new component using other components; it works like other frameworks' composition, macro expansion, or inline replacement functionality. In ZK, defining and using macro components takes three steps:

1. Define a macro component using a ZUML page:

```
<hbox>Username: <textbox/></hbox>
```

    2.   Declare the macro component in the page that is going to use it:

```
<?component name="username" macro-uri="/WEB-INF/macros/username.zul"?>
```

    3.   Use the macro components, which is no different from using other components:

```
<window>
 <username/>
</window>
```

Note ➡ As the number of components in the macro component increases, keeping identifiers unique becomes increasingly difficult. Thus, the macro component itself is, by default, an independent ID space in order to avoid the problem of identifier conflict.

Integrating Mega Components

In addition to a variety of native GUI components, ZK has integrated some famous Ajax components such as Google Maps, FCKeditor, and Dojo. They are used no differently that other ZK components.

Google Maps

Google Maps is fully supported by ZK. Google uses some tricks in loading their Maps Javascript API code, so you have to sign up for the Google Maps API (http://www.google.com/apis/maps/) to get your web site a key before you can use the maps; if you don't register, you will not be able to access the Google Maps database.

After getting the key, copy it and paste it in place of ABQIAAA . . . in script shown in Listing 4-19. Then, you can generate a mapfor your web page using Google Maps by declaring a <gmaps/> tag using ZMUL. To see an example, you could copy Listing 4-19 into a .zul page and visit this page with a browser.

Listing 4-19. Example of Google Maps

```
<window>
<script type="text/javascript" src="http://maps.google.com/maps?file=api&amp; ➡
v=2&amp;key=ABQIAAAAmGxmYR57XDAbAumS9tV5fxTwMObrOpm-All5BF6Poa ➡
KBxRWWERSynObNOWSyMNmLGAMZAO1WkDUubA"/>
<gmaps width="500px" height="300px" showSmallCtrl="true"/>
</window>
```

Note ➡ The script embedded in this example includes a key for using the Google Maps API. It is only effective for the following host: http://localhost:8080/.

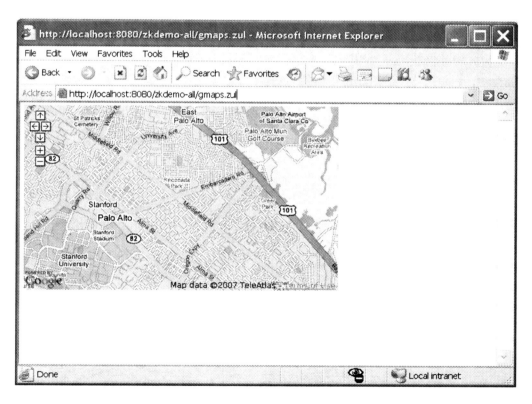

Figure 4-6. Using Google Maps on a ZUML page

FCKeditor

FCKeditor is a well-known online rich text editor; you can use <fckeditor/> to incorporate FCKeditor into your web page. As an example, you could declare a web page with this line:

```
<fckeditor height="300px"/>
```

Figure 4-7 shows what you will see on the screen. There are numerous buttons for effects to enrich the text. You can type words in the panel, highlight those words, and click any of the buttons to change the look of your words.

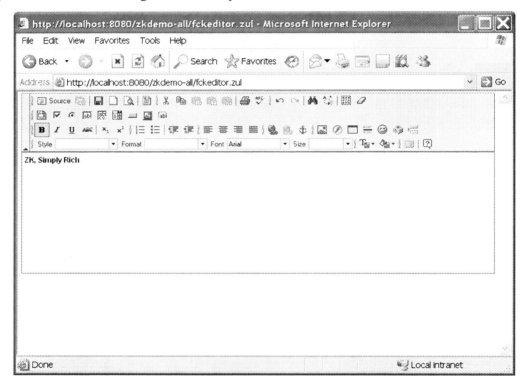

Figure 4-7. FCKeditor can be integrated into your ZUML pages as well.

Dojo

Next, I am going to introduce you a major player in Ajax frameworks—the Dojo JavaScript library. Listing 4-20 shows one the most famous uses of Dojo, a fish-eye list which viewing a list of images with a fisheye zooming in. You could give it a try by creating the page in Listing 4-20 and mousing over the icons on the screen.

Note ➡ For more information about Dojo, visit the URL: http://dojotoolkit.org/.

Listing 4-20. An Example Using Dojo to Create a Fish-EyeList

```
<zk>
  <fisheyelist id="fi" style="position:absolute;margin:20px" ➡
attachEdge="top">
    <fisheyeitem image="/img/icon_browser.png"
     label="Web Browser" onClick="alert(self.label)"/>
    <fisheyeitem image="/img/icon_calendar.png"
     label="Calendar" onClick="alert(self.label)"/>
    <fisheyeitem image="/img/icon_email.png"
     label="Email" onClick="alert(self.label)"/>
    <fisheyeitem image="/img/icon_texteditor.png"
     label="Text Editor" onClick="alert(self.label)"/>
    <fisheyeitem image="/img/icon_update.png"
     label="Software Update" onClick="alert(self.label)"/>
    <fisheyeitem image="/img/icon_users.png"
     label="Users" onClick="alert(self.label)"/>
  </fisheyelist>
  <div height="200px" width="100%" style="border:1px solid black;"/>
</zk>
```

When you mouse-over an icon, that icon will grow bigger, as shown in the leftmost icon in Figure 4-8.

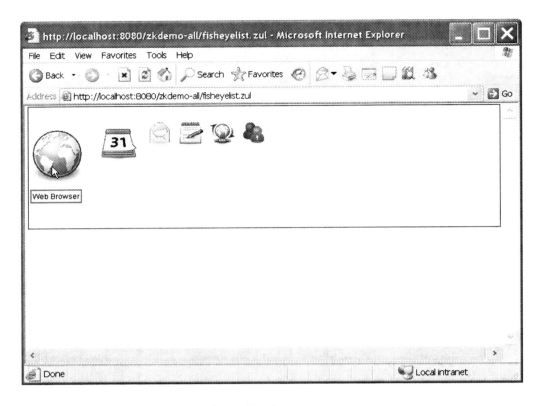

Figure 4-8. A menu using the Dojo fish-eye list feature

Summary

This chapter has introduced you many tools for building ZK components, as well as to the life cycle of ZUML pages and components and how ZK implements the idea of event-driven programming. In addition, this chapter explored some of the mega components supported by ZK—Google Maps, FCKeditor, and Dojo. Though these ideas are easy to understand, ZK makes using them quick and easy too.

In the next chapter, I am going to guide you through building your first web application with ZK. Let's see how easy it is.

PART 2

■■■

Applying Your ZK Knowledge

In this part, you will learn how to develop real web applications with a Java SE architecture using the ZK Framework and a light-weight servlet container. I will walk through various important parts with a real web application with you and explain why it is implemented that way. Learning by example is always the fastest way to understand a framework.

CHAPTER 5

Setting Up the Development Environment

This chapter tells you how to prepare your development environment for building a ZK Ajax web application. You should follow these steps to set up an environment for developing ZK applications:

1. Install the most recent JDK.

2. Install Tomcat.

3. Install the Eclipse IDE software development kit (SDK)

4. Set up the .zul file extension in the XML editor.

5. Configure ZK to work with Eclipse.

Once your development environment is all set up, I'll introduce you to a few more handy tools for use with the ZK Framework.

Installing the Java SE (JDK)

First of all, you should install a Java Development Kit (JDK) as described in Chapter 2. The most updated version now is Java SE 6. If you have a previously installed JDK already, be aware that ZK requires at least JDK 1.4. However, I strongly recommend you to install at least Java SE 5 (which uses JDK 1.5); you will experience fewer problems of incapability between it and Tomcat 5.5+.

Installing Tomcat

Recall from Chapter 2 that a Java servlet container (a web container) is also required for running ZK applications. ZK also requires EL expression support, which has been available since Java Servlet 2.4, so you should install Tomcat 5.5 as instructed in Chapter 2. Remember to write down your Tomcat installation directory (the default is C:\Program Files\Apache Software Foundation\Tomcat 5.5), HTTP/1.1 connector port (the default is 8080), and administrator login user name (the default is admin) and password (the default is empty).

Note ➡ We will call the Tomcat installation directory $TOMCAT in this book.

Installing the Eclipse IDE SDK

After setting up the JRE and Tomcat server, I strongly recommend that you install Eclipse, another IDE that has many convenient tools for developing applications. Among Java IDEs, Eclipse is the most popular, and it supports a lot of powerful plug-ins, especially the WebTools Platform (WTP) designed for developing Java EE 5 applications. WTP includes a source editor for XML, HTML, JSP and others; a J2EE project builder; a build-in browser; and more.

Though installing Eclipse is not required to use the ZK Framework, having the same development environment as mine may reduce the number of minor errors caused by inconsistencies across development environments. Use the instructions in the following section to install Eclipse with the WTP.

Downloading Eclipse with WTP

Go to http://download.eclipse.org/webtools/downloads/drops/R1.5/R-1.5.4-200705021353/, select to download Eclipse WebTools Platform; All-in-one, and install it. It is easy to install Eclipse: just unzip the downloaded file to a directory, for example, C:\eclipse. Please write down your installation directory, which is called $ECLIPSE in this book. Eclipse WTP includes all the required tools and plug-ins to develop a web application.

Specifying the Workspace for Eclipse

Before you start using Eclipse, you need to specify the workspace for storing your applications as follows:

1. Go to your Eclipse root installation directory, $ECLIPSE (for example, C:\eclipse).

2. Double-click the eclipse.exe icon shown in Figure 5-1.

Figure 5-1. The Eclipse icon

3. The Workspace Launcher dialog box will pop up; use it to set up your workspace, which is the place to keep your Java code and configuration files. I suggest using the suggested directory unless you want to keep your code somewhere else. Remember your workspace directory name (it will be called $WORKSPACE in this book).

Setting Up Tomcat to Work with Eclipse

Eclipse supports a variety of application servers. To make Eclipse work with Tomcat, you need to set up Tomcat as a runtime server for running web applications:

1. From the Eclipse menu, select Window ➤ Preferences.

2. The Preferences dialog window will open; see Figure 5-2. In the tree menu on the left, select Server ➤ Installed Runtimes. Then click the Add button. You should see a New Server Runtime dialog window pop up.

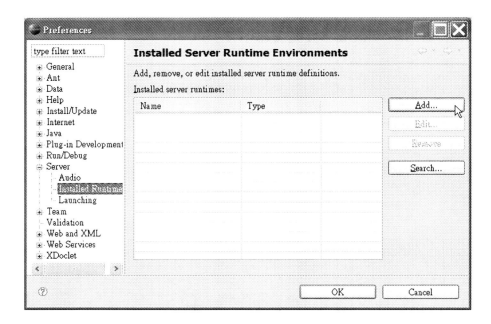

Figure 5-2. In the Preferences dialog box, select Server, followed by Installed Runtime.

3. In the New Server Runtime dialog shown in Figure 5-3, select Apache ➤ Apache Tomcat v5.5, and click the Next button.

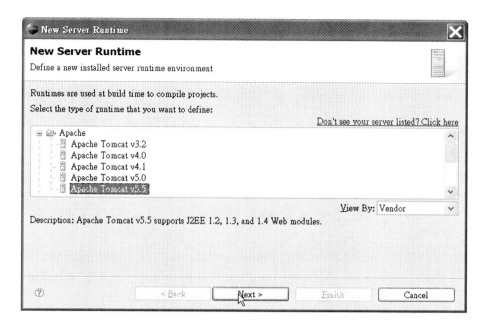

Figure 5-3. Select your server in the New Server Runtime dialog.

4. Browse to and select your Tomcat root directory, $TOMCAT (for example, C:\Program Files\Apache Software Foundation\Tomcat 5.5); see Figure 5-4. Next, select your JRE (for example, jre 1.6.0), and click the Finish button.

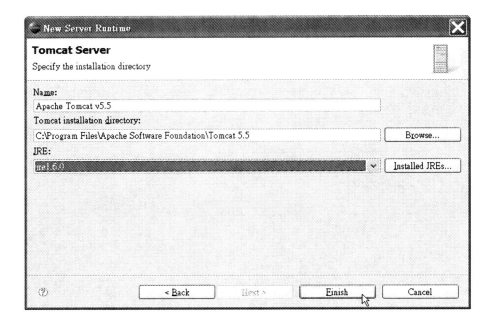

Figure 5-4. Select your root directory and JRE before clicking Finish.

5. Click the OK button in the Preferences dialog box.

Defining a Server Instance

After setting up Tomcat as a runtime server, you need to define a server instance of Tomcat to use for deploying web applications:

1. From the Eclipse menu, select Window ➤ Show Views ➤ Others. You should see the Show View dialog box pop up.

2. In the Show View dialog box (see Figure 5-5), select Server ➤ Servers, and click the OK button.

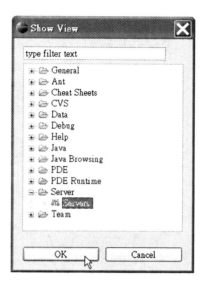

Figure 5-5. In the Show View dialog box, click Server and then Servers.

3. Under the Servers tab, right-click to show the context menu. Select New ➤ Server as shown in Figure 5-6. You should see the New Server dialog window pop up.

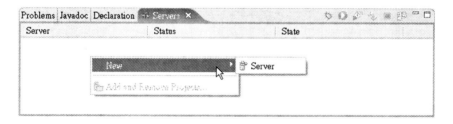

Figure 5-6. Right-click to display the context menu.

4. In the New Server dialog box shown in Figure 5-7, you will define your new server. In the "Server's host name" field, enter **localhost**. In the "Select the server type" field, choose Tomcat v5.5 Server. Then, in the "Server runtime" field, select Apache Tomcat v5.5. Finally, click the Finish button.

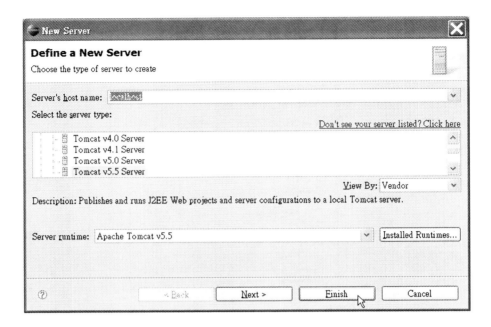

Figure 5-7. Specify the details of your server in the New Server dialog box.

Setting Up the .zul File Extension in the XML Editor

As mentioned before, Eclipse provides an XML editor. To use the XML editor to develop a ZK application, you need to associate .zul file extension with the XML editor. Follow these instructions to establish the association:

1. From the Eclipse menu, select Window ➤ Preferences. You should see the Preferences dialog box pop up.

2. From the tree menu on the left side of the Preferences dialog box, select General ➤ Content Types. You should see the Content Types pane appear.

3. In the Content Types pane, select Text ➤ XML, and click the Add button (see Figure 5-8). You should see New File Type dialog box pop up.

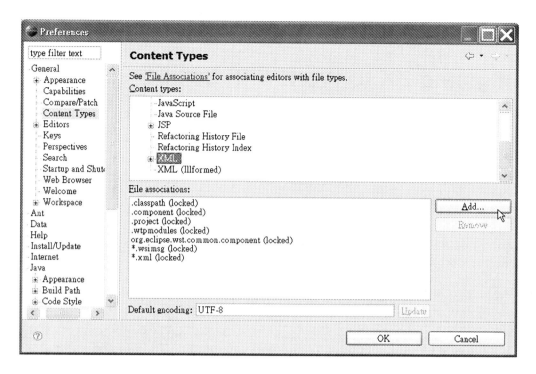

Figure 5-8. Select the content type for Eclipse from the Preferences dialog box.

4. In New File Type dialog box's "File type" field, type ***.zul**, and click the OK button (see Figure 5-9).

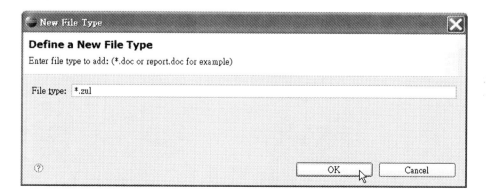

Figure 5-9. Defining a new file type

5. Click the OK button in Preferences dialog box.

Configuring ZK to Work with Eclipse

Finally, it's time for us begin developing a web application. In the following sections, I will tell you how to develop a ZK web application with Eclipse, run this application, and use a built-in browser to view the results.

Creating a Dynamic Web Project

First of all, you should choose the project type and create the dynamic web application. The instructions are as follows:

1. From the Eclipse menu, select File ➤ New ➤ Project. You should see a New Project dialog box pop up.

2. From the New Project dialog box, select Web ➤ Dynamic Web Project, and click the Next button, as shown in Figure 5-10. You should see the New Dynamic Web Project dialog box pop up.

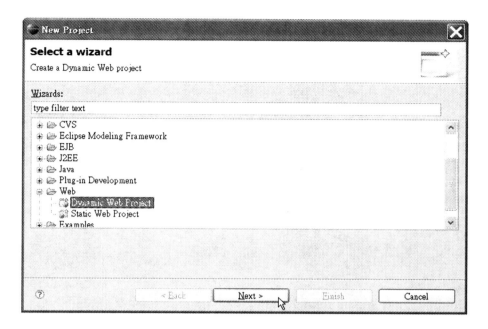

Figure 5-10. Choose your project type in the New Project dialog box.

3. In the New Dynamic Web Project dialog box's "Project name" field, enter your new
    project name. For practice, type **hello** now, and click the Finish button (see Figure 5-
    11). Eclipse will create a folder with the project name (in our example, hello) under
    your Eclipse workspace. We will call the directory of this folder, $PRJ (for example,
    c:\eclipse\workspace\hello) later in this book.

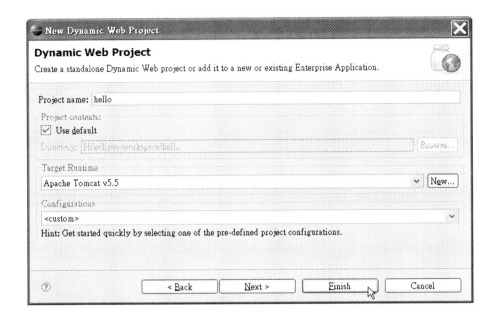

Figure 5-11. Give your project a name in the New Dynamic Web Project dialog box.

Importing ZK JAR Libraries and Setting Up Web Configurations

For developing a ZK web application, we need some resources and configuration. Specifically, you'll need to import the required JAR files for running a ZK application and configure the web.xml and zk.xml files under the $TOMCAT\WEB-INF server. Follow these steps to do so:

1. Download the ZK binary, zk-x.y.z.zip, at http://www.zkoss.org/download/ (x.y.z is the ZK version number).

2. Unpack your zk-x.y.z.zip file to a temporary folder, say, C:\zk-x.y.z.

3. Copy the zk-x.y.z/dist/lib/*.jar files to your $PRJ/WebContent/WEB-INF/lib directory.

4. Copy the zk-x.y.z/dist/lib/ext/*.jar files to your $PRJ/WebContent/WEB-INF/lib directory.

5. Copy the zk-x.y.z/dist/lib/zkforge/*.jar files to your $PRJ/WebContent/WEB-INF/lib directory.

Note ➡ Functions of these JAR files were explained in Chapter 2; please refer to "Relative Libraries."

---

6. Copy zk-x.y.z/demo/src/zkdemo/WebContent/WEB-INF/web.xml to your $PRJ/WebContent/WEB-INF/ directory and overrides the original web.xml.

7. Copy zk-x.y.z/demo/src/zkdemo/WebContent/WEB-INF/zk.xml to your $PRJ/WebContent/WEB-INF/zk.xml directory.

8. From the Eclipse Project Explorer view, right-click the project's WebContent to show the context menu. Select Refresh to make Eclipse associate the copied files (see Figure 5-12).

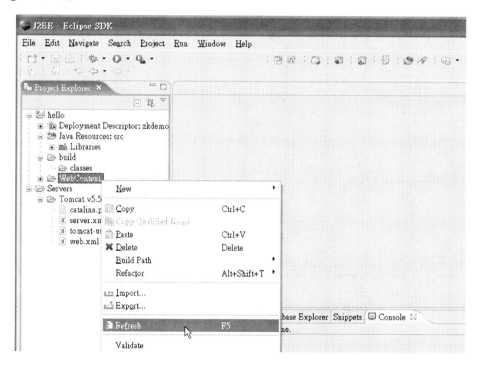

Figure 5-12. Refresh the WebContent option in Project Explorer view to complete the configuration.

9. The copied libraries should now be shown under Java Resources:src ➤ Libraries ➤ Web App Libraries in Project Explorer view.

Creating a New index.zul File

Let's create your very first application with Eclipse, and, of course, it is a Hello World application.

1. From the Eclipse Project Explorer view, right-click the project's WebContent to show the context menu. Select New ➤ File; you should see the New File dialog box pop up.

2. In the New File dialog box's "File name" field, type **index.zul**, and click the Finish button (see Figure 5-13).

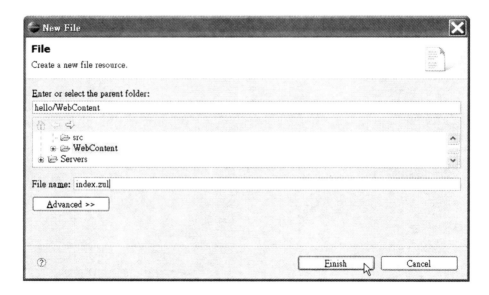

Figure 5-13. Give your project file a name in the New File dialog box.

3. Click the Source tab on the lower-left corner of the middle pane, and type the following lines, which create a simple Hello World application, into index.zul. Save the file by pressing Ctrl+S.

```
<window title="hello" border="normal" width="200px">
  Hello World!
</window>
```

Caution ➡ If you have not associated the .zul file extension with the XML editor, you will receive an "Unsupported Content Type" error message from Eclipse.

Running Your First Application

Next, we are going to deploy the Hello World application on Tomcat and see the results of running it. Running this simple application could be used to verify your Tomcat configuration. Deploy the application as follows:

1. From the Eclipse Project Explorer view, select WebContent ➤ index.zul, and right-click to show the context menu.

2. From the context menu, select Run As ➤ Run on Server. Click the Next button. The Hello World project should appear in the left pane; add it to the right pane to import this project to Tomcat, and click the Next button. You should see the Select Tasks dialog box pop up.

3. In the Select Tasks dialog box, shown in Figure 5-14, check the "Update context root for Web module hello" check box, and click the Finish button.

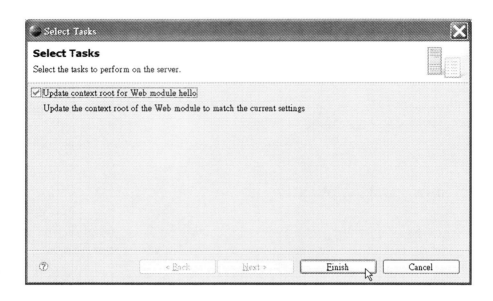

Figure 5-14. Choose to update the context root of your application in the Select Tasks dialog box.

4. The Tomcat server will start and Eclipse's embedded browser will open and automatically point to http://localhost:8080/hello/index.zul. You should see the ZK hello window shown in Figure 5-15 in the browser.

Figure 5-15. Your first application in action

More Convenient Tools

Now that you've got your first application up and running, I am going to introduce you to a couple of additional convenient tools for developing and debugging ZK applications, including ZK source code, and a XML schema.

Importing ZK Source Code into Eclipse

When with a running application throws an exception, it would be best if we could see the source code that caused it; that would save a lot time in eliminating the bug. So in this section, I am going to tell you how to import ZK source code into Eclipse for more efficient debugging:

1. Create a new subfolder under your Eclipse workspace folder called something like $WORKSPACE/zksrc.

2. Copy zk-x.y.z/dist/src/*.jar to your $WORKSPACE/zksrc folder.

3. Select Java Resources:src ➤ Libraries ➤ Web App Libraries ➤ zcommon.jar, and right-click to show the context menu. Select Properties as shown in Figure 5-16. You should see the Properties dialog box for zcommon.jar pop up.

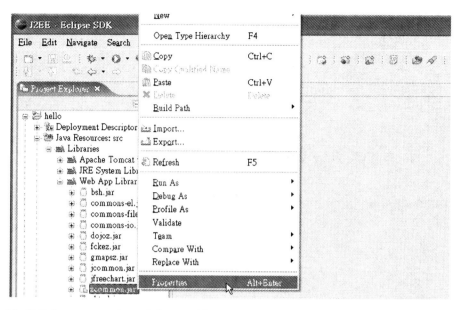

Figure 5-16: Editing properties of the jar file

4. In the Properties dialog box, select Java Source Attachment. Click the External File button adjacent to the "Location path" field to pick the associated source JAR file. In this case, it is $WORKSPACE/zksrc/zcommon-source.jar.

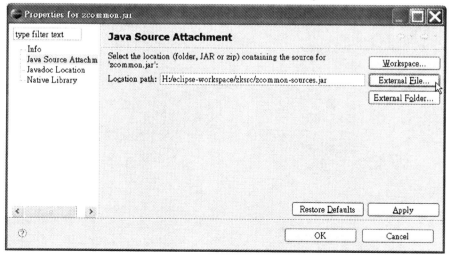

Figure 5-17: Import source code of the jar file

5. One by one, right-click the project's other ZK JAR files, which are shown in the following list, and attach the Java source code to each, as illustrated in steps 3–4. When you import the source code to the source library, the library automatically reformats the name xxx.jar to xxx-source.jar, so it is fairly straightforward.

- zhtml.jar

- zkplus.jar

- zk.jar

- zul.jar

- zkweb.jar

Integrating the zul.xsd XML Schema

An *XML schema* defines a set of rules to which XML documents must conform, and an XML schema definition (XSD) is an instance of an XML schema. An XSD is useful for finding illegal XML declarations. It also gives you XML definition hints while you're developing an application, by listing all definitions of this XSD file automatically in Eclipse, which is particularly useful to those who are not familiar with XML schema. Great news—ZK already contains an XSD file, and I'm going to guide you through importing that file, *zul.xsd, into Eclipse:

1. From the Eclipse menu, select Window ➤ Preferences, and you should see the Preferences dialog window pop up.

2. From the Preferences window, select Web and XML ➤ XML Catalog, as shown in Figure 5-18. You should see the XML Catalog panel appear.

3. In the XML Catalog Entries field, select User Specified Entries, and click the Add button. You should see the Add XML Catalog Entry dialog box pop up.

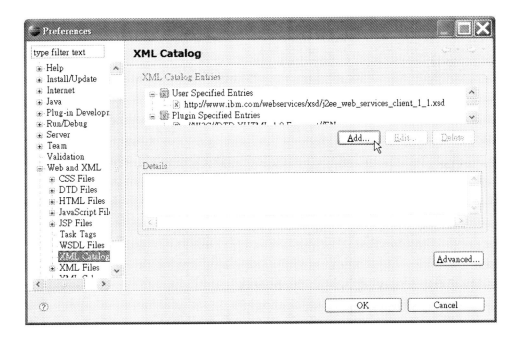

Figure 5-18. Add the XSD file in the Preferences dialog box.

4. In the Add XML Catalog Entry dialog box's URI field, type
http://www.zkoss.org/2005/zul/zul.xsd, as shown in Figure 5-19. In the Key Type
field, select Schema Location. In the Key field, type
http://www.zkoss.org/2005/zul/zul.xsd. Click the OK button.

Note ➡ zul.xsd contains XML definitions of ZK components.

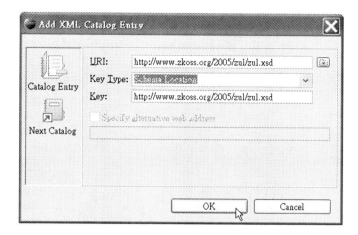

Figure 5-19. In the Add XML Catalog Entry dialog box, assign the URI, key type, and key name for the new XSD.

5. Now you should see a new entry, http://www.zkoss.org/2005/zul/zul.xsd, under User Specified Entries in the XML Catalog panel.

6. Click the OK button to close the Preferences dialog box.

Creating a Page Using the zul.xsd XML Schema

Now that you've integrated the XSD file into Eclipse, let's develop a simple application with the help of the XML schema. In this example, you'll experience the convenience of developing an application with automatic hints.

1. From the Eclipse menu, select File ➤ New ➤ Other, and you should see the New dialog box pop up.

2. From the New dialog window, select XML ➤ XML from the tree menu, and click the Next button, as shown in Figure 5-20. You should see the first page of the Create XML File wizard pop up.

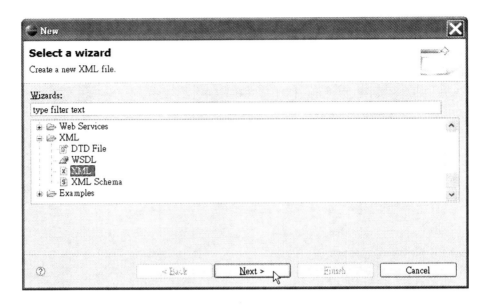

Figure 5-20. Choose to create a new XML file in the New dialog box.

3. On the Create XML File page of the wizard, select the "Create XML file from an XML schema file" radio button, and click the Next button, as shown in Figure 5-21. You should see the XML File Name page pop up.

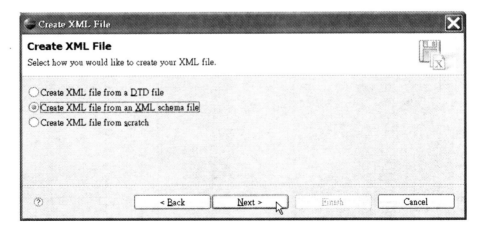

Figure 5-21. Opt to use an XML schema file in the Create XML File dialog box.

4. On the XML File Name page, shown in Figure 5-22, type or select the parent folder for your project. It is generally in the WebContext folder of your project. Then type in the ZUL file name you want to create (for example, hello.zul) and click the Next button to move on to the Select XML Schema File page.

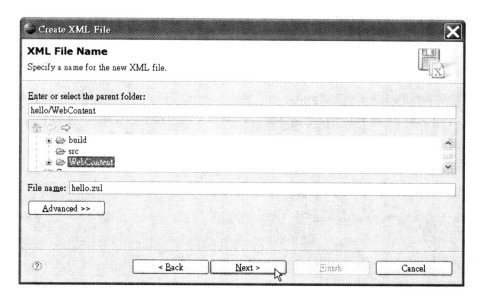

Figure 5-22. Specify the names of the parent folder and XML file on the XML File Name page.

5. From the Select XML Schema File page, shown in Figure 5-23, select the "Select XML catalog entry" radio button; you should see the http://www.zkoss.org/2005/zul/zul.xsd file in the XML Catalog list. Select that entry, and click the Next button to move on to the Select Root Element page.

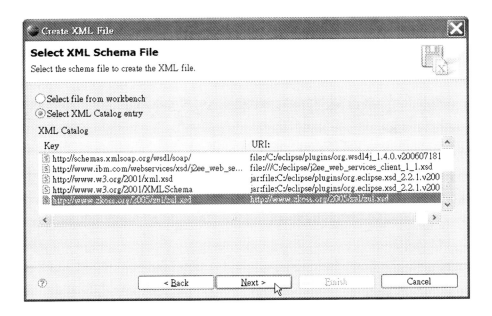

Figure 5-23. Select your XSD file on the Select XML Schema File page.

6. On the Select Root Element page, in the "Root element" field, pick the root element. In most ZK applications, it is a window or zk element. For this example, choose zk (see Figure 5-24). Leave the Content options section as it is, and click the Finish button.

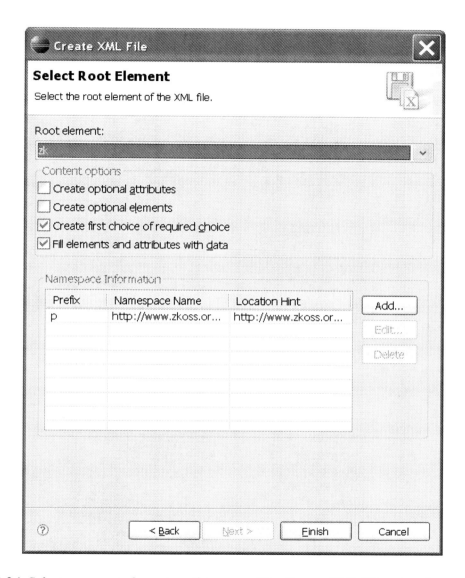

Figure 5-24. Select your root element on this page of the Create XML File wizard.

7. The ZUL file is created and opened in an XML editor window. Click the Source tab in the lower left corner of the middle pane to change the view.

8. Now you can start editing your ZUL file. Press Alt+/ to open the Content Assistant window as shown in Figure 5-25 to help you fill up proper ZUL elements and attributes.

Figure 5-25. The Content Assistant window lists all ZUL elements.

Patching a Lost xsd URL in Eclipse

If your attempt to import zul.xsd fails, it may be caused by a file that Sun has lost. If you run into this problem, use the following steps to solve it:

1. Download http://java.sun.com/xml/ns/j2ee/j2ee_web_services_client_1_1.xsd, and save the file to your Eclipse installation directory, $ECLIPSE (for example, C:\eclipse).

2. From the Eclipse menu, select Window ➤ Preferences to open the Preferences dialog box.

3. In the Preferences dialog box, select Web and XML ➤ XML Catalog, and click the Add button. You should see the Add XML Catalog Entry dialog box pop up.

4. In the Add XML Catalog Entry dialog box, click the browse icon next to the URI field, and choose File System to open a file explorer dialog box.

5. In the file explorer, select the j2ee_web_services_client_1_1.xsd file you just downloaded and saved, and click the Open button. The file explorer will close, and the full file path of j2ee_web_services_client_1_1.xsd should appear in the URI field of the Add XML Catalog Entry dialog box.

6. Back in the Add XML Catalog Entry dialog box, the Key Type field should show NameSpace Name. Keep it as it is.

7. In the Add XML Catalog Entry dialog box's Key field, type **http://www.ibm.com/webservices/xsd/j2ee_web_services_client_1_1.xsd**.

8. Click the OK button.

Summary

In this chapter, you spent a lot of time learning to use an IDE to develop a web application. An IDE provides numerous convenient tools for developing and debugging. I hope this is helpful for you as you work through the examples in subsequent chapters—I don't want you to have to spend too much time compiling, debugging, deploying, and running the projects.

In next chapter, I'll introduce a well-know Ajax web application from Sun, and I'll show you how to replace the UI with a ZK one.

CHAPTER 6

Creating a Real Web Application

In the previous chapter, you should have prepared your Eclipse IDE for developing a ZK Ajax web application. In this chapter, I will show you how to implement a real ZK web application step by step, so you can see the whole life cycle of developing a web application with ZK.

The ZK web application I am going to show you how to build is based on the famous Java Pet Store 2.0 reference application, developed by the BluePrints program at Sun Microsystems.

Introducing Java Pet Store 2.0

Before we dive into creating our ZK pet shop application, let's take a look at the Java Pet Shop. Java Pet Store 2.0 is designed to illustrate how the Java Platform, Enterprise Edition 5 (Java EE 5), and JavaServer Faces (JSF) can be used to develop an Ajax-enabled Web 2.0 application. It provides a sample meeting ground for buyers and sellers of pets. If you are interested in learning more about this application, you can download the Java Pet Store from this URL:

http://java.sun.com/developer/releases/petstore/

Creating the ZK Pet Shop Application

In this web application, I am going to throw away the heavy Java EE 5 platform and instead use lightweight technologies. For example, the EJB 3 persistent technology used in the Java Pet Store 2.0 will be replaced with a Hibernate persistent layer. And, of course, for the GUI parts, I will replace the JavaServer Faces technology with the ZK Ajax presentation framework.

Since ZK Pet Shop application is built based on the model, view, controller (MVC) architecture, I would like to give you a brief explanation of this architecture:

- *Model*: Represents the information used in an application
- *Viewer*: The presentation layer of data (also know as the user interface)
- *Controller*: The processes for responding to events, often user's actions, and a bridge between the data model and the viewer

To avoid confusing our application with the Java Pet Store, I would like to name the ZK application that we're going to build "ZK Pet Shop."

Installing ZK Pet Shop

First of all, I recommend that you install ZK Pet Shop and play around with the application to better understand how it works, and you could take a look at the source code if you'd like to. Follow these instructions to install ZK Pet Shop:

1. Download zkPetShop.zip, and unzip it.

2. Open Eclipse.

3. From the Eclipse File menu, select Import.

4. In the pop-up dialog box, select Web ➤ WAR file, and click Next.

5. Click the Browse button in the upper-right corner to specify the location of zkPetShop.war, and click the Finish button.

6. Activate the Tomcat server in Eclipse.

7. Open a browser to visit this URL: http://localhost:8080/zkPetShop

8. Copy the petshop folder to the root directory of the same disk drive as the Eclipse workspace.

Note ➡ In the following sections, I extract code snippets from zkPetShop for explanation, but most of them couldn't be tested alone as they appear in the text. Please refer to the zkPetShop file for the complete source code.

Creating the Home Page of ZK Pet Shop

The home page of ZK Pet Shop, shown in Figure 6-1, is defined in the index.zul page; it includes a fish-eye list and a parrot with pet icons, and each of these provides a hyperlink to catalog.zul for browsing pet information. The banner for this page is defined in another page, banner.zul.

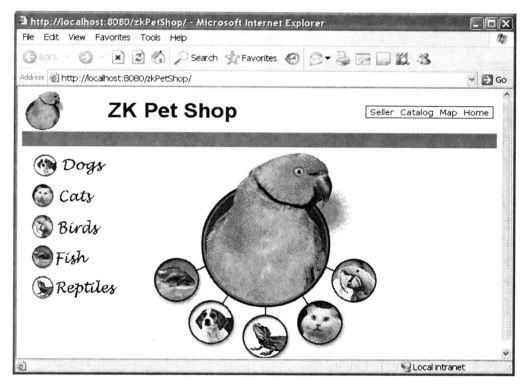

Figure 6-9. The index.zul page (The pet images in this figure are from the Java Pet Store application.)

Building a Fish-Eye List with Dojo

Building a list with a fish-eye lens effect using Dojo in ZK is easy compared with building the one in the Java Pet Store application, because ZK provides an easy way to create a the list using ZUML without having to code any JavaScript. Listing 6-1 is a code snippet extracted from index.zul. The fish-eye list is defined by a <fisheyelist> tag, and there are a lot of properties to define the behavior and appearance of this list. Each child component of the fish-eye list is defined by a <fisheyeitem> tag, and the image property allows you to assign an image file for each of the child fisheyeitem components.

Note ➡ For more information about the Dojo toolkit, visit this URI: http://dojotoolkit.org/

Listing 6-1. The Fish-Eye List in index.zul

```
<fisheyelist id="fi" itemWidth="170" itemHeight="50"
    itemMaxWidth="340" itemMaxHeight="100"
    itemPadding="10"
    attachEdge="left" labelEdge="right"
    orient= "vertical">
<fisheyeitem image="/images/dogs_icon.gif" onClick='go("DOGS")'/>
<fisheyeitem image="/images/cats_icon.gif" onClick='go("CATS")'/>
<fisheyeitem image="/images/birds_icon.gif" onClick='go("BIRDS")'/>
<fisheyeitem image="/images/fish_icon.gif" onClick='go("FISH")'/>
<fisheyeitem image="/images/reptiles_icon.gif"
onClick='go("REPTILES")'/>
</fisheyelist>
```

Tables 6-1 and 6-2 show the most commonly used attributes of the fisheyelist and fisheyeitem components and their functions.

Table 6-1. Attributes of fisheyelist

Attribute	Function
itemWidth	Sets the width of fisheyeitem
itemHeigh	Sets the height of fisheyeitem
itemMaxWidth	Sets the maximum width of fisheyeitem
itemMaxHeight	Sets the maximum height of fisheyeitem
attachEdge	Defines which edge of fisheyeitem the zoom appears to zoom toward
labelEdge	Defines which edge of fisheyeitem any labels in the list will be rendered on

Table 6-2. Attributes of fisheyeitem

Attribute	Function
image	Sets the image for this item
onClick	Registers an onClick event listener

Listening for an onClick Event

When the user clicks any pet icon in the list, we have to transfer from this page to the catalog.zul page, which displays the photos and descriptions for the type of pet chosen by the user. Therefore, we have to register an onClick event listener for each listitem to invoke the go() method; this method transfers the user from the home page to the page of catalog.zul corresponding to the pet icon the user clicks.

In Listing 6-2, the go() method is defined within the <zscript> tag, and it passes the catid, which represents the category of pet, as a parameter. Then, the Executions.sendRedirect() method transfers from the home page to catalog.zul accordingly.

Listing 6-2. The go Method in index.zul

```
<zscript>
 void go(String catid) {
    if (catid != null) {
      if ("BIGBIRDS".equals(catid))
        catid = "BIRDS";
        Executions.sendRedirect("catalog.zul?catid="+catid+"#0");
  }
 }
</zscript>
```

Building an Image with Hyperlinks

In addition to clicking a list item to be redirected to catalog.zul, the user could also click one of the pet icons surround the green parrot. First of all, we need to insert the pet image files onto index.zul and build hyperlinks to each of these pet icons.

Listing 6-3 is a code snippet extracted from index.zul. This snippet creates an image imagemap component, and uses its src property to specify the source of the image file—the green parrot surrounded with other pets' icons in home page.

Secondly, we use the area component to locate the region of each of the pet icons in this image file. The position, range, and shape of area is defined by its coordinates (coords) attribute. An area component supports three kinds of shapes: circle, polygon, and rectangle. In this example, we pass four parameters into coords, so the shape of each area is a square, and its range is defined by those coordinates. And, the tooltiptext attribute of area sets the message to show when the user mouses over the area.

Note ➡ The coordinates of the mouse position are screen pixels counted from the upper-left corner of the image beginning with (0, 0).

Listing 6-3. Adding imagemap to index.zul

```
<imagemap src="/images/splash.gif" tooltiptext="Pet Selection Map"
width="350" height="355" onClick="go(event.area)">
    <area id="BIGBIRDS" tooltiptext="Birds" coords="72,2,280,250"/>
    <area id="FISH" tooltiptext="Fish" coords="2,180,72,250"/>
    <area id="DOGS" tooltiptext="Dogs" coords="60,250,130,320"/>
    <area id="REPTILES" tooltiptext="Reptiles" coords="140,270,210,340"/>
    <area id="CATS" tooltiptext="Cats" coords="225,240,295,310"/>
    <area id="BIRDS" tooltiptext="Birds" coords="280,180,350,250"/>
</imagemap>
```

Finally, the way to add hyperlinks onto those icons is registering an onClick event listener in imagemap to invoke the go() method and passing event.area as a parameter, which specifies the id of the pet icon clicked by the user.

Including banner.zul in index.zul

We still need to attach the banner to the ZK Pet Shop application, so let's do so now. The banner.zul page contains a small icon of parrot in the upper-left corner, the title of this application in the middle, and a menu bar in the upper-right corner, as shown in Figure 6-2.

The include component is used to insert the output generated by another servlet into your page; the servlet could be created with anything, including JSF, JavaServer Pages

(JSP), or even another ZUML page, and the src property is used to specify the location of the page generating the output. Include banner.zul in index.zul as follows:

```
<include src="banner.zul"/>
```

 ZK Pet Shop   Seller Catalog Map Home

Figure 6-2. The banner.zul page (The parrot icon in this figure is from the Java Pet Store application.)

Adding the Parrot Icon

In Listing 6-4, the parrot icon is referenced as an image component, and it registers an onClick event listener to redirect the user to index.zul page—by invoking Executions.getCurrent().sendRedirect("/index.zul")—when the user clicks this icon.

Listing 6-4. banner.zul

```
<div width="100%">
 <hbox valign="middle" width="100%">
<image src="/images/banner_logo.gif" width="70px" height="70px"
onClick='Executions.getCurrent().sendRedirect("/index.zul")'
</image>
    <space spacing="20px"/>
  <label class="banner" value="ZK Pet Shop"/>
    <space spacing="40px"/>
    <menubar style="float:right;">
      <menuitem  label="Seller" href="/seller.zul"/>
      <menuitem  label="Catalog" href="/catalog.zul#0"/>
      <menuitem  label="Map" href="/mapAll.zul"/>
      <menuitem  label="Home" href="/index.zul"/>
    </menubar>
 </hbox>
</div>
<div width="100%" height="24px" style="background-color: gray">
</div>
<separator/>
```

Note ➡ A separator is used to insert a space between two components. A space is a variant of separator whose default orientation is vertical. The hbox component is used to create a horizontally oriented box. Each component placed in the hbox will be placed horizontally in a row.

Adding the Title

The title of this application is defined in a label component with "ZK Pet Shop" as its value, as follows:

```
<label class="banner" value="ZK Pet Shop"/>
```

The class property indicates a cascading style sheet (CSS) definition for the style of the title's label. Listing 6-5 shows the CSS definitions of the banner class, which is defined within a pair of style tags.

Listing 6-5. banner CSS Definition for the Title's label

```
<style>
.banner {
  height:35px;
  font-size:35px;
  font-weight: bold;
  font-family: Arial
}
</style>
```

Adding the Menu Bar

To build the menu bar in banner.zul, you simply declare a menubar component and its children, menuitem components. One thing to remember is that the style component could be used in any kind of UI component to define the component's style. In Listing 6-6, the style of the menu bar is defined directly within the style property of menubar.

In addition, within each menuitem component, there are two properties: label sets the text on it, and href sets its corresponding hyperlink.

Listing 6-6. menubar in banner.zul

```
<menubar style="float:right;">
      <menuitem  label="Seller" href="/seller.zul"/>
      <menuitem  label="Catalog" href="/catalog.zul#0"/>
      <menuitem  label="Map" href="/mapAll.zul"/>
      <menuitem  label="Home" href="/index.zul"/>
</menubar>
```

Requirements for the ZK Pet Shop Application

Here are the three main requirements that we are going to implement:

- Allow the user to publish information about pets for sale.

- Allow the user to browse pet information and photos.

- Allow the user to search for a pet's location with Google Maps.

First, I will focus on the viewer and controller and how they interact with each other according to user's activities.

Interaction Between Viewer and Controller

In the architecture of MVC, the presentation layer and business logic is separated into viewer and controller. The communication between these two is frequent, since the controller needs to render data into the viewer or get data from the viewer.

Besides, the viewer has to invoke the methods defined in controller to respond to users' actions. Thus, to make the interaction between viewer and controller simple, we should satisfy the following two conditions while building this application:

- The viewer can easily invoke methods defined in the controller.

- The controller can easily render or get data from the viewer.

How could we implement this application to satisfy those requirements? No doubt, ZK itself is the viewer, but how do we build the controller? The best practice is to replace the viewer's default window class with a customized one as a controller of this application, so that we can define required resources, methods, and initiations in this customized class. The benefit is that all of the children components in the customized window component could invoke methods defined in it by its reference ID directly. In addition, it is easy for the window component (controller) to get its child components, since they are in the same ID space—the customized window component (controller) simply invokes getFellow() to get its children components to retrieve or refresh their content.

All three of our main requirements are accomplished by the cooperation between the viewer and controller, as explained in the following sections.

Publishing Information About Pets

To fulfill this requirement, we should provide a viewer for the user to submit his pet's information (seller.zul) and a controller that is responsible for collecting data from the viewer and saving it in a database (org.zkforge.petshop.controller.SellerWindow).

Most of the control code is defined in the SellerWindow class, including preparing required data and saving a user's submission into database.

Creating seller.zul

In the seller.zul page, we provide a way for the user to publish information about a pet that's for sale, including the pet's information and the seller's information. For this, we are going to need the following features:

- A form for submitting pet information
- A rich text editor for formatting the pet description
- The ability to upload the pet's photo
- A form for submitting the seller's contact information
- CAPTCHA for verification
- Client-side validation of the user's submission
- The ability to save the user's submission into a database

Note ➡ CAPTCHA is trademarked by Carnegie Mellon University (http://www.captcha.net/).

Declaring the Controller for seller.zul

First, let's replace the default window class with the customized org.zkforge.petshop.controller.SellerWindow class. For this, ZK provides the use attribute; use will replace the default class of any component with a customized class. The following declaration is extracted from seller.zul page, and all attributes and methods defined in org.zkforge.petshop.controller.SellerWindow could be retrieved by its reference id ("win"):

```
<window id="win" use="org.zkforge.petshop.controller.SellerWindow">
```

Creating a Form for Submitting Pet Information

Figure 6-3 shows the form for a user to submit a pet's information.

Figure 6-3. The "Information about your pet" form in seller.zul (The parrot icon in this figure is from the Java Pet Store application.)

The form is like a table, so I chose the grid component to represent it. A grid contains components that are aligned in rows. Inside a grid, you declare two things, the columns, which define the header and column attributes, and the rows, which provide the content. Each row in this grid represents a field of pet's information. The code to create the grid for the "Information about your pet" form is shown in Listing 6-7.

Listing 6-7. A Form for Submitting Pet's Information

```
<grid>
 <columns>
  <column width="250px"/>
  <column/>
 </columns>
 <rows>
 <row spans="2">
<div align="center">
<label style="font-weight:bold;" value="Information about your pet"/>
</div>
</row>
 <row>Category:
<listbox id="products" mold="select" rows="1"/>
</row>
 <row>*Pet's name:
<textbox id="petName"/>
</row>
 <row>*Description(3 lines max):
<fckeditor id="description" customConfigurationsPath="/seller.js" ➡
toolbarSet="seller" height="100px">
</fckeditor>
</row>
 <row>*Price(In US dollars):
<decimalbox id="price" format="$#,##0.00"/>
</row>
 <row>
  <hbox>*Image File:
  <button id="image" label="upload" onClick="win.upload()"/>
  </hbox>
  <image id="picture" width="100px" height="77px"/>
</row>
</rows>
</grid>
```

Adding the Rich Text Editor

The rich text editor is implemented using the well-know online text editor FCKeditor, which is also integrated in ZK. However, the default setting of FCKeditor includes more functions than our Pet Shop application needs. Since we only need basic functions like modifying the text's font and color, we need to customize the toolbar of the fckeditor component:

1. Create seller.js under the root path of zkPetShop.

2. Create a new toolbar set in seller.js using the following line:

```
FCKConfig.ToolbarSets["seller"] = ➡
[['Bold','Italic','Underline','StrikeThrough','-','TextColor', ➡
'BGColor']] ;
```

3. Specify sell.js as a parameter of the customConfigurationsPath attribute of the fckeditor component, and specify "seller" as the toolbarSet attribute.

```
<fckeditor id="description" customConfigurationsPath="/seller.js"➡
toolbarSet="seller" height="100px"/>
```

Note ➡ For more information on FCKeditor, visit the project's web site: http://www.fckeditor.net/

Providing the File Upload Functionality

In the ZK Pet Shop, when the user clicks the "upload" button, a dialog box pop up prompting the user to upload the file. After uploading, a pet's icon appears in the right cell of the "upload" button, showing the image uploaded by the user.

Listing 6-8 creates the "upload" button and registers an onClick event listener that invokes the win.upload() method when the button is clicked by the user. The win.upload() method renders a small icon of the pet's photo uploaded by the user into the image component.

Listing 6-8. Using a Button to Upload an Image File

```
<row>
<hbox>*Image File:
    <button id="image" label="upload" onClick="win.upload()"/>
</hbox>
    <image id="picture" width="100px" height="77px"/>
</row>
```

Listing 6-9 shows the win.upload() method. win.upload() invokes the Fileupload.get() method that retrieves the image file, stores the file's content as an img object, and uses the picture.setContent() method to put this image file to the image component defined in Listing 6-8.

Listing 6-9. Defining win.upload

```
public void upload() {
  Image picture = (Image) getFellow("picture");
  try {
   Object img = Fileupload.get();
     if (img instanceof org.zkoss.image.AImage) {
      picture.setContent((AImage)img);
     } else if (img != null) {
Messagebox.show("Not an image: "+img, "Error",➡
Messagebox.OK, Messagebox.ERROR);
     }
       _img = (AImage) img;
     } catch (InterruptedException e) {
       throw UiException.Aide.wrap(e);
     }
  }
}
```

Note ➡ The org.zkoss.zul.Fileupload class provides utilities to allow a user to upload a file from the browser. The get method shows a dialog that prompts the user to specify the file to upload.

Creating a Form for Submitting a Seller's Contact Information

Next, we need to add the "Information about yourself" form shown in Figure 6-4 for the seller to submit contact information.

Figure 6-4. The "Information about yourself" form in seller.zul (The parrot icon in this image is from the Java Pet Store application.)

The structure of this form is much the same as the pet information form; it is constructed with a grid component, and each piece of the seller's contact information is represented as a row component.

Listing 6-10. A Form for Submitting the Seller's Contact Information

```
<grid>
 <columns>
  <column width="250px"/>
  <column/>
 </columns>
 <rows>
  <row spans="2">
<div align="center">
<label style="font-weight:bold;" value="Information about yourself"/>
</div>
</row>
<row>*First Name:<textbox id="firstName"/></row>
<row>*Last name: <textbox id="lastName"/></row>
  <row>Seller Email: <textbox id="email"/></row>
  <row>*Street: <textbox id="street" cols="50"/></row>
  <row>*City: <textbox id="city"/></row>
  <row>*State: <textbox id="state"/></row>
  <row>*ZipCode: <textbox id="zipCode"/></row>
  <row>
   <vbox>
   Enter the text as it is shown below (case insensitive)
   <captcha id="captcha" length="5" noise="false"/>
   </vbox>
   <textbox id="verify" constraint="No Empty" maxlength="5"/>
  </row>
 </rows>
</grid>
```

Note ➡ The vbox component is used to create a vertically oriented box. Added components will be placed underneath each other in a column.

Adding a CAPTCHA

Now that we've collected the pet and seller information, we need to add a CAPTCHA to make sure this submission is send by human before saving it into the database. Since ZK supports a CAPTCHA component, we can simply declare a captcha component with

ZUML. In Listing 6-11, a `captcha` component is used to dynamically generate distorted text; it takes the following attributes:

- length: Used to set the length of the text string

- noise: Determines whether to create extra disturbance in the text of this CAPTCHA

Listing 6-11. Adding the CAPTCHA

```
<vbox>
Enter the text as it is shown below (case insensitive)
<captcha id="captcha" length="5" noise="false"/>
</vbox>
```

Adding Client-Side Validation Constraints

In order to make sure the user's data submission meets our data format requirements, ZK supports the constraint component for specifying acceptable formats for input values. The constraint component can be a property of the textbox component, which we used to allow user input. The parameters of constraint should be a regular expression or a predefined string of ZK; for example, setting a text box's constraint to the string no empty means that the form cannot be submitted without a value in that box.

Note ➡ A *regular expression* is a string used for matching a set of words according to predefined syntax. There is a tutorial in using regular expression on Sun's website (http://java.sun.com/docs/books/tutorial/essential/regex/).

In the pet information form, let's suppose that the "Pet's name" field only accepts English letters, so constraint="/.[a-zA-Z]+/" is added as a property of the textbox of petName as follows:

```
<row>*Pet's name: <textbox id="petName" constraint="/.[a-zA-Z]+/"/></row>
```

If the user types an illegal character, such as a number, an error message will be displayed on the right side of this field when the user clicks the mouse away from the field.

In the seller's contact information form, each of the fields has a corresponding constraint component, as shown in Listing 6-15.

Listing 6-12. Validation Constraints for the Seller's Contact Information

```
<row>*First Name:
<textbox id="firstName" constraint="/.[a-zA-Z]+/" /></row>
<row>*Last name:
<textbox id="lastName" constraint="/.[a-zA-Z]+/" /></row>
<row>Seller Email:
<textbox id="email" constraint="/.+@.+\.[a-z]+/"/></row>
<row>*Street:
<textbox id="street" cols="50" constraint="/.[a-zA-Z0-9]+/"/></row>
<row>*City:
<textbox id="city" constraint="/.[a-zA-Z]+/"/></row>
<row>*State:
<textbox id="state" constraint="/.[a-zA-Z]+/"/></row>
<row>*ZipCode:
<textbox id="zipCode"/></row>
<row>
 <vbox>
Enter the text as it is shown below (case insensitive)
     <captcha id="captcha" length="5" noise="false"/>
  </vbox>
 <textbox id="verify" constraint="No Empty" maxlength="5"/>
</row>
```

Figure 6-5 demonstrates the result when the user's submission fails validation.

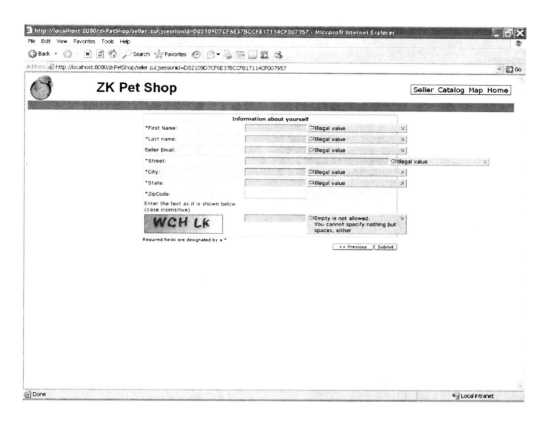

Figure 6-5. Constraint error messages (The parrot icon is from the Java Pet Store application.)

Note ➡ If you prefer to display a customized message instead of the default one, you could amend the constraint with colon followed by the message you want to display, for example: <textbox constraint="/.+@.+\.[a-z]+/: e-mail address only"/>

Saving the User's Submission in a Database

Before saving the user's submission, we should confirm two things: whether the user passed the CAPTCHA validation and whether the user submitted an image file. The code to confirm these items is shown in Listing 6-13.

Listing 6-13. Confirming the CAPTCHA Validation and Image Upload

```
public void submit() {
Textbox tbxverify = (Textbox)getFellow("verify");
  String verify = tbxverify.getValue();
  Captcha captcha = (Captcha)getFellow("captcha");
if (!captcha.getValue().equalsIgnoreCase(verify)) {
    try {
Messagebox.show("Incorrect verify string, try type the charcter ➡
in the image.", "Error", Messagebox.OK, Messagebox.ERROR);
    } catch (InterruptedException e) {
      throw UiException.Aide.wrap(e);
    } finally {
      captcha.randomValue(); //change a value for next try
    }
      return;
    }
  if (_img == null) {
    try {
Messagebox.show("Please upload your pet picture.", "Error",➡
Messagebox.OK, Messagebox.ERROR);
    } catch (InterruptedException e) {
      throw UiException.Aide.wrap(e);
    }
      return;
  }
```

Secondly, we should retrieve all of the user's submission data by invoking the getFellow() method shown in Listing 6-14.

Listing 6-14. Retrieving Data from the Viewer

```
//pet info
  Listbox lbx = (Listbox)getFellow("products");
    Product product = (Product) getProducts().get(lbx.getSelectedIndex());
    String productId = product.getProductID();
  String petName = ((Textbox)getFellow("petName")).getValue();
  String description = ((FCKeditor)getFellow("description")).getValue();
  BigDecimal price =((Decimalbox)getFellow("price")).getValue() ➡
.setScale(2, BigDecimal.ROUND_HALF_UP);
    String tags = ((Textbox)getFellow("tags")).getValue();
  //contact info
  String firstName = ((Textbox)getFellow("firstName")).getValue();
  String lastName = ((Textbox)getFellow("lastName")).getValue();
```

```
String email = ((Textbox)getFellow("email")).getValue();
//seller's address
String street1 = ((Textbox)getFellow("street")).getValue();
String city = ((Textbox)getFellow("city")).getValue();
String state = ((Textbox)getFellow("state")).getValue();
String zip = ((Textbox)getFellow("zipCode")).getValue();
```

The last step is to save everything into the database by invoking the catalogFacade.addItem(item) method shown in Listing 6-15.

Listing 6-15. Saving Data into the Database

```
SellerContactInfo contactInfo = new SellerContactInfo ➡
(firstName, lastName, email);
    Item item = new Item(productId,petName,description, ➡
pictureURL,thumbURL,price,addr,contactInfo,0,0);
    Long itemId = catalogFacade.addItem(item);
```

Note ➡ org.zkforge.petshop.model.catalogFacade is a façade class responsible for communicating with Hibernate to access the database.

Browsing Pet Information and Photos

Now that the user can save information about pets that are for sale, we can move on to the second requirement of our application: the ability to browse pet information. To accomplish this, we need to provide a viewer for the user to browse pet information and photos and a controller that is responsible for retrieving pet data from the database and refreshing the content of user interface components according to the user's activities. The viewer will be in catalog.zul and the controller in org.zkforge.petshop.controller.CatalogWindow.

Updating catalog.zul

The catalog.zul page shown in Figure 6-6 is composed of the following four parts:

- A menu bar on the left side
- A large photo of pet on the right side
- A pane beneath the large photo to show the detailed description of that pet
- A gallery of other pet images beneath the description pane

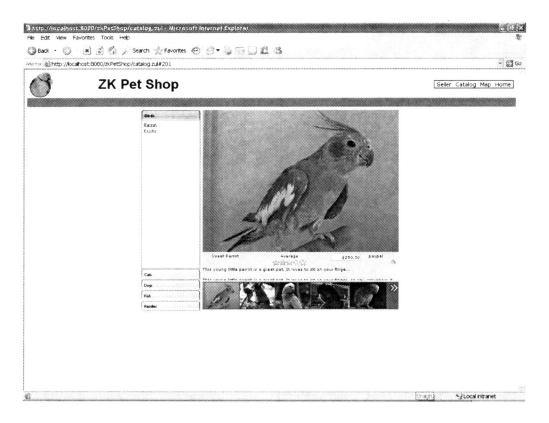

Figure 6-6. The catalog.zul page (This pet icons on this page are from the Java Pet Store application.)

Creating the Menu Bar

The menu bar is composed of two parts: the pet categories and type of pets available in the selected category, the pet products. In this menu bar, each category is represented as a tab, and pet products are listed on the pane below the tab; only one pane can be open at a time.

The `tabbox` component provides the functionality for implementing a menu of grouped components in which only one group needs to be available at once, so we'll create the menu bar as a `tabbox`. Each pet category and its available pets are represented by a group of components, as shown in Listing 6-17.

Listing 6-17. Adding the tabbox Component to catalog.zul

```
<tabbox id="cattbx" width="150px" mold="accordion">
<tabs>
  <tab forEach="${categories}" id="${each.categoryID}"➧
 label="${each.name}" selected="${each.categoryID == catID}"/>
</tabs>
    <tabpanels>
    <tabpanel forEach="${categories}" height="380px" >
    <vbox>
    <zscript>
      import org.zkforge.petshop.model.CatalogFacade;
      List tmpproducts = new CatalogFacade().getProducts(each.categoryID);
    </zscript>
  <toolbarbutton forEach="${tmpproducts}" label="${each.name}"➧
tooltiptext="${each.description}">
    <attribute name="onClick">{
      import org.zkforge.petshop.model.Item;
String pID = self.getAttribute("productID");
      List items = catalogwin.getItems(pID);
      Item item = items.get(0);
      catalogwin.refreshThumbs(items);
      catalogwin.refreshItem(item);
    }</attribute>
    <custom-attributes productID = "${each.productID}"/>
    </toolbarbutton>
    </vbox>
    </tabpanel>
  </tabpanels>
 </tabbox>
```

Each tab component in tabbox represents one kind of pet's category. Each tab component is composed of the following component:

- tab: Each tab represents one category of pets

- tabpanel: The body of a tab panel, includes the pets available in the category

- toolbarbutton: Each toolbarbutton represents one kind of pet

When the user clicks any tab in this tabbox, the menu will switch to display the tab chosen by the user and show the pets available in that category on the pane.

In Listing 6-18, instead of declaring tab components one by one for all of the pet categories, the forEach attribute is adopted to create tab components automatically according to the specified objects. We assign categories, a collection of category objects, as a parameter to forEach property using EL expression.

Listing 6-18. foreach Attribute

```
<tabs>
<tab forEach="${categories}" id="${each.categoryID}"➽
label="${each.name}" selected="${each.categoryID == catID}"/>
</tabs>
<tabpanels>
  <tabpanel forEach="${categories}" height="380px">
</tabpanels>
```

Next, we need to create buttons for each of the available pets in the tab panels using the toolbarbutton component; see Listing 6-19. For each toolbarbutton, we should get each available pet's name and description from the database by its categoryID. We also have to register an onClick event listener for each toolbarbutton to refresh the large image and all of the small pet images in the gallery to match the pet product clicked by the user.

Listing 6-19. Adding toolbarbutton Compoents to tabpanel

```
<tabpanel forEach="${categories}" height="380px" >
 <vbox>
 <zscript>
    import org.zkforge.petshop.model.CatalogFacade;
List tmpproducts = new CatalogFacade().getProducts(each.categoryID);
  </zscript>
<toolbarbutton forEach="${tmpproducts}" label="${each.name}" ➽
tooltiptext="${each.description}">
      <attribute name="onClick">{
    import org.zkforge.petshop.model.Item;
String pID = self.getAttribute("productID");
List items = catalogwin.getItems(pID);
Item item = items.get(0);
    catalogwin.refreshThumbs(items);
    catalogwin.refreshItem(item);}
</attribute>
<custom-attributes productID = "${each.productID}"/>
   </toolbarbutton>
</vbox>
</tabpanel>
```

When the user clicks any toolbarbutton on the pane, all of data for that pet is retrieved from the database by sending the productID chosen by the user to catalogwin.getItems(pID). The catalogwin.refreshThumbs(items) and catalogwin.refreshItem(item) methods are invoked to refresh the content of both the large and thumbnail photos of the pets.

Creating the Large Photo

The large photo is defined in catalog.zul as follows:

```
<div height="375px" style="overflow:hidden">
<image id="bigimage" width="500px" height="375px" src="${item.imageURL}"/>
</div>
```

Creating the Gallery of Pet Thumbnail Images

To implement a gallery of thumbnail images, first of all, we use an hbox component as a container for the images in which each of pet's thumbnail is represented as an image component. Also, an items variable, which is a collection item objects, is assigned as an object of a forEach attribute to automatically create the image components.

Then, each thumbnail image component is registered with a customized onClick event listener defined in the CatalogWindow class; when the onClick event is invoked, it replaces the large pet photo with the pet shown in the thumbnail clicked by the user. In addition, we put this hbox under a div component to show only the first five pets' thumbnails (the div component serves as a picture frame). See Listing 6-20 for the code to implement the gallery.

Listing 6-20. Creating the Gallery

```
<div id="outid" style="overflow:hidden;background-color:#546474; ➥
position:relative;" width="500px" height="74px">
<hbox id="inid" spacing="2px" style="position:relative;top:2px; ➥
background-color: #546474;left:0px;">
<image src="${each.imageThumbURL}" height="70px" ➥
style="cursor:pointer;" forEach="${items}">
    <custom-attributes item="${each}"/>
    <zscript>
      self.addEventListener("onClick", selectItemListener);
    </zscript>
</image>
</hbox>
</div>
```

Note ➡ custom-attributes is a convenient way to assign attributes to components directly without programming.

Now, we need to provide the user a way to see the rest of icons placed in this hbox, so we'll use double arrows as in the Java Pet Store application. To make the arrows functional, we need the help of JavaScript, and the action attribute is used to call functions defined in JavaScript. The syntax of the action attribute is as follows, and multiple definitions are allowed:

action="[onfocus|onblur|onclick|onshow|onhide|...]: javascript function;"

Listing 6-21 defines the two sets of arrows: one pointing to the right and the other pointing to the left.

Listing 6-21. Adding Arrows to Scroll the Photo Gallery

```
<div id="leftid" style="cursor:pointer;float:left; ➡
position:relative;top:-65px;" tooltiptext="Show Previous Items" ➡ visible="false">
<image src="/images/left.gif" action="onmouseover:move(#{outid}, ➡
#{inid}, #{leftid}, #{rightid}, true);onmouseout:stop();"/>
</div>
<div id="rightid" style="cursor:pointer;float:right; ➡
position:relative;top:-65px;"  tooltiptext="Show More Items">
<image src="/images/right.gif" action="onmouseover:move(#{outid}, ➡
 #{inid}, #{leftid}, #{rightid}, false);onmouseout:stop();"/>
</div>
```

Note ➡ In the JavaScript code, you can reference ZK components or other objects with the late-binding EL expression. The late-binding EL expression starts with #{ and ends with } as depicted in Listing 6-21.

In this example, a JavaScript function called move(#{outid} is triggered when the user mouses over either of the arrows, and stop() is invoked when the user moves the mouse away from the arrows.

Creating the Description Pane

Just above the gallery of images is a pane that shows a short description of the pet featured in the large photo, and the pane can be pulled up to show more information about this pet by clicking the up-facing arrow. Slideup() and Slidedown() are two JavaScript functions to pull up and push down this pane.

Listing 6-22. Adding functionality to the Arrows of the Shadow Pane

```
<vbox>
<space spacing="5px"/>
<image id="up" src="/images/up.gif" tooltiptext="Show Details" ➥
action="onclick:slideup(#{info}, #{down}, #{up})" ➥
style="cursor:pointer;"/>
<image id="down" src="/images/down.gif" tooltiptext="Show Less ➥
Details" action="onclick:slidedown(#{info}, #{down}, #{up})" ➥
visible="false" style="cursor:pointer;"/>
</vbox>
```

Searching for a Pet's Location with Google Maps

Recall that the third main requirement for our ZK Pet Shop application is the ability to map the location of pets for sale. To meet this requirement, in the viewer, we should provide a form for the user to submit a query and a Google Map for showing the queried location. The controller is responsible for getting the pet's data from the database in response to the user's query and refreshing the content of the components in the viewer. The viewer for this functionality is mapall.zul, and the controller is org.zkforge.petshop.controller.MapWindow.

Creating mapall.zul

The main requirements of this page are to provide a way for the user to search for a pet's location by address and to show the search result on Google Maps. To satisfy these requirements, the following tasks should be accomplished:

- Create a form for submitting user's address as a query
- Provide the ability to search for pet locations in the database

• Show the pet locations with Google Maps

Creating a Form for Submitting an Address as a Query

Figure 6-7 shows a form to search for nearby pets by typing an address and specifying the category of pet and search range. If the user clicks the Map Category button, the search result will be shown using Google Maps and a table, which will be explained in the next two sections.

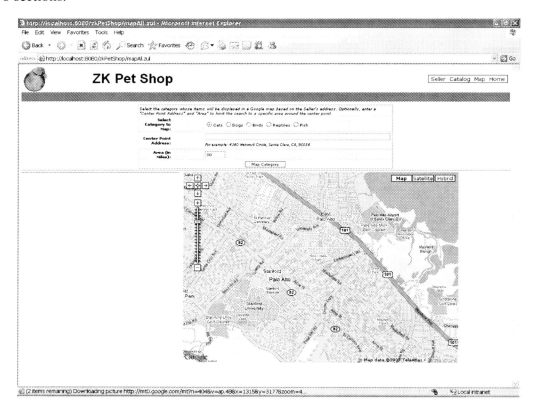

Figure 6-7. The mapall.zul page (The parrot icon is from the Java Pet Store application.)

The query form is itself a grid component (see Listing 6-23). Each row in the grid represents a field in the query form. The radiogroup component is adopted, since only one of its child components can be selected at a time. Thus, each of pets' categories is represented as a radio component. In addition, textbox and intbox components are used for the user to type the address and search range.

Listing 6-23. Creating the Query Form

```
<grid>
<columns>
    <column width="80px" align="right"/>
    <column/>
</columns>
  <rows>
    <row spans="2">
        <div align="left">
        <label style="font-style:italic; font-size: normal" ➥
value="Select the category whose items will be displayed ➥
in a Google map based on the Seller's address. Optionally, ➥
enter a &quot;Center Point Address&quot; and &quot;Area&quot; ➥
to limit the search to a specific area around the center point."/>
        </div>
        </row>
        <row>
        <label style="font-weight:bold" value="Select Category to Map:"/>
        <radiogroup id="rgroup">
    <radio id="CATS" label="Cats" checked="true"/>
    <radio id="DOGS" label="Dogs"/>
    <radio id="BIRDS" label="Birds"/>
    <radio id="REPTILES" label="Reptiles"/>
    <radio id="FISH" label="Fish"/>
  </radiogroup>
  </row>
    <row>
        <label style="font-weight:bold" value="Center Point Address:"/>
        <vbox width="100%">
      <textbox id="caddr" width="98%"/>
<label style="font-style:italic;font-size:xx-small;" ➥
value="For example: 4140 Network Circle, Santa Clara, CA, 95054"/>
        </vbox>
    </row>
        <row>
        <label style="font-weight:bold" value="Area (in Miles):"/>
    <intbox id="radius" constraint="no negative, no zero" value="30" ➥
  cols="7"/>
    </row>
    <row spans="2">
    <div align="center">
```

```
    <button label="Map Category" onClick="win.showItems()"/>
    </div>
    </row>
  </rows>
</grid>
```

Using Google Maps to Show Pet Locations

Google Maps is fully supported by ZK. To use Google Maps, you should first register for a key on the Google Maps API web site (http://www.google.com/apis/maps/). Recall that Google requires you to register to get your web site a key before you can access the Google Maps database.

After getting your key, copy it and paste in place of ABQIAAAA . . . in <script ... key=ABQIAAA . . ."> as shown in Listing 6-24.

Listing 6-24. The script Component for Using Google Maps

```
<script type="text/javascript" src=http://maps.google.com/maps? ➥
file=api&amp;v=2&amp;key=ABQIAAAAmGxmYR57XDAbAumS9tV5fxTwM0brOpm- ➥
AII5BF6PoaKBxRWWERSynObNOWSyMNmLGAMZAO1WkDUubA
/>
```

Note ➥ The key in Listing 6-24 is only effective for the URL: http://localhost:8080. A script component is used to declare script codes running at the client. It is the same as HTML SCRIPT tag.

In order to generate the map using your Google maps key, you simply declare a gmap component and register an onMapClick event listener to respond to the user's request (see Listing 6-25).

Listing 6-25. gmap

```
<gmaps id="maps" width="700px" height="500px" showLargeCtrl="true" ➥
showTypeCtrl="true" onMapClick="win.showInfo(event)"/>
```

When the user clicks the Map Category button, the win.showItems() method is called and many red hot-air balloons appear on the map to indicate locations of pets. Google Maps in action is shown in Figure 6-8.

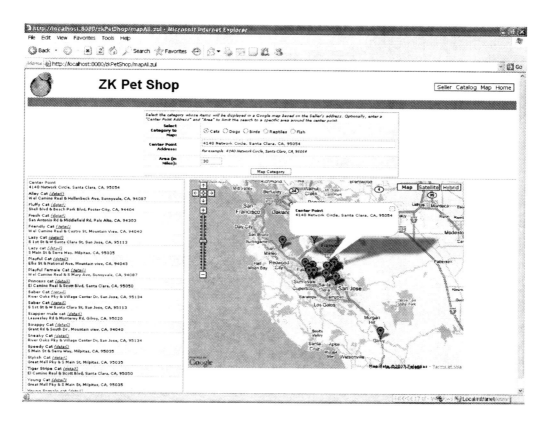

Figure 6-8. Google Maps in action (The parrot icon is from the Java Pet Store application.)

Showing the Result with Google Maps

As shown in Figure 6-16, the search result is comprised of two parts: pets' locations and pets' information.

The requirements for accomplishing these two types of search results are as follows:

- Show the pets' locations on a gmap component

- Show the pets' information in a grid component

Showing Pets' Locations on the gmap **Component**

The first step is to set the address submitted by the user as the center of Google Maps by invoking maps.setCenter(dLatitude, dLongitude). dLatitude and dLongitude represent the latitude and longitude coordinates of the user's address, as shown in Listing 6-27.

Listing 6-27.Set the Center of gmap

```
Gmaps maps = (Gmaps) getFellow("maps");
maps.setCenter(dLatitude, dLongitude);
```

Next, add the first Gmarker on the map you just invoked. You need to prepare the latitude and longitude coordinates of the pet's address and the message shown in the bubble above its red balloon:

1. Create a Google marker (Gmarker) component with a message and location data:

```
Gmarker marker = new Gmarker(changeSpaces(infoBalloon), dLatitude, ➡
dLongitude);
```

2. Give an ID to this Gmarker for further processing:

```
marker.setId("center");
```

3. Activate this Gmarker:

```
marker.setOpen(true)
```

4. Attach this Gmarker to the Google Maps instance you invoked:

```
marker.setParent(maps);
```

Showing Pets' Information in the gr id

Each row in the grid component presents the following information:

- Pet's name (detail)
- Pet's address

Each row in the grid is composed of two label components—pet's name and pet's address—and one toolbarbutton component (detail). The functions of this grid are to

• Redirect this page to the catalog.zul page when the user clicks the "detail" link

- Indicate the pet's location on the map when the user clicks its row in the grid
- Show the pet's details and thumbnail photo in a pop-up window when the user mouses over its row in the grid

Redirecting this Page to catalog.zul

When the user clicks the "detail" link, this page will be redirected to the catalog page for the selected pet (catalog.zul where ItemID indicates that pet). The following snippet drives the "details" link; tb.setHref("catalog.zul#"+loc.getItemID()) establishes a hyperlink to catalog.zul# with the appropriate ItemID:

```
//detail
Toolbarbutton tb = new Toolbarbutton("(detail)");
tb.setHref("catalog.zul#"+loc.getItemID());
tb.setStyle("font-style: italic;");
tb.setParent(div);
```

Indicating the Pet's Location on the Map

In Listing 6-29, both the title and address of each pet are registered with an onClick event listener with a customized MarkerListener, and a marker attribute is added into their attributes. The marker attribute indicates the ID of Gmarker. In addition, a tooltip component is added to make it possible to show a pet's details when the user mouses over its row.

Listing 6-29. Adding the onClick Event Listener to Each Row

```
    //title
MarkerListener listener = new MarkerListener();
org.zkoss.zul.Label label = new org.zkoss.zul.Label(title);
label.addEventListener("onClick", listener);
label.setStyle("cursor: pointer");
label.setAttribute("marker", "marker"+ii);
label.setTooltip("info");
label.setParent(div);

//address
    label = new org.zkoss.zul.Label(addressstr);
    label.addEventListener("onClick", listener);
    label.setStyle("font-size:xx-small;cursor: pointer");
    label.setAttribute("marker", "marker"+ii);
```

```
label.setTooltip("info");
label.setParent(div);
```

Customizing the Event Listener

To implement an EventListener component in ZK, you must implement the onEvent()
methods. Processing defined in onEvent() will be executed when the event is triggered.

In Listing 6-30, when the user clicks any pet in this grid, the event listener for that pet's
marker (MarkerListener) will open the Gmarker matching the specified pet with the ID
defined as a marker attribute of the pet's title and address.

Listing 6-30. Adding MarkerListener

```
private static class MarkerListener implements EventListener {
    public void onEvent(Event event) {
org.zkoss.zul.Label label = (org.zkoss.zul.Label) ➥
        event.getTarget();
    String id = (String)label.getAttribute("marker");
    if (id != null) {
     Gmarker marker = (Gmarker) label.getFellow(id);
     if (marker != null) {
       marker.setOpen(true);
      }
     }
    }
   }
```

Showing the Pet's Details and Thumbnail Photo in a Pop-Up Window

When the user mouses over any text in the row of grid, the pop-up window shown in Figure
6-9 appears.

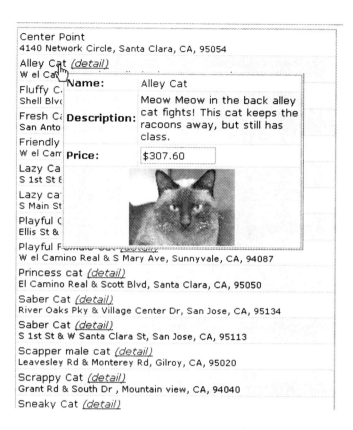

Figure 6-9. Pop-up window (The image in this figure is derived from the Java Pet Store application.)

To show the pet's details and thumbnail image in a pop-up window, define the popup component in mapall.zul page as follows:

```
<popup id="info" width="300px" onOpen="win.whenPopup(event)"/>
```

When the user clicks a row in the grid, this popup component will open, and the onOpen event listener will be triggered to invoke the win.whenPopup(event) method, as shown in Listing 6-31.

After that, evt.getReference() retrieves the component (label component) that invoked the onOpen event and gets information about the pet from a item attribute defined in its parent component (row component). Then, an item variable is stored in an arg HashMap. The last step is to invoke Executions.createComponents() to create the components defined in the popup.zul page, indicating the popup component as the parent component and passing arg as a parameter to be retrieved in the popup.zul page.

Note ➡ arg is the type of java.util.Map that is be used to transmit data to another ZUL page dynamically created using Execustions.createComponents().

Listing 6-31. whenPopup()

```
public void whenPopup(OpenEvent evt){
    if (evt.isOpen()) {
      Component x = (Component) evt.getReference();
      Item loc = (Item) x.getParent().getAttribute("item");
      Popup popup = (Popup) evt.getTarget();
      popup.getChildren().clear();
      Map arg = new HashMap(1);
      arg.put("item", loc);
      Executions.createComponents("/popup.zul", popup, arg);
    }
  }
```

Note ➡ The createComponents() method in the org.zkoss.zk.ui.Executions class creates only components, not pages, even though it loads a ZUML file (that is, a page).

Creating popup.zul

The components in the popup.zul page are defined in Listing 6-32: the pet's name, description, price, and thumbnail image. All of the required data is retrieved via the arg variable transmitted from the previous popup component with an EL expression.

Listing 6-32. The popup.zul Page

```
<grid >
<rows>
<row>
<label style="font-weight:bold" value="Name:"/>
<label value="${arg.item.name}"/>
</row>
```

```
<row>
<label style="font-weight:bold" value="Description:"/>
<html content="${arg.item.description}"/>
</row>
<row>
<label style="font-weight:bold" value="Price:"/>
<decimalbox readonly="true" format="$#,##0.00" ➡
value="${arg.item.price}" />
</row>
<row spans="2">
<div align="center">
<image src="${arg.item.imageURL}" height="100px"/>
</div>
</row>
</rows>
</grid>
```

Note ➡ arg is a map of parameters that could be accessible by the arg variable in EL Expression.

This is the last part of the rich GUI, and you've accomplished an Ajax web application with ZK. Though it is intuitive to develop this application using ZK , which is component-based and event-driven, I strongly recommend that you look back at Chapter 4, which discussed a lot about the life cycles of the desktop, page, and components. You will acquire deeper understanding about ZK and be able to develop another application more rapidly.

Summary

In this chapter, I've introduced you briefly to the Java Pet Store application, and then we created the ZK Pet Shop application, which replaces the Java GUI with a ZK one. The ZK Pet Shop requires less effort to implement Ajax-enabled web pages than the Java EE 5 store, since you no longer have to write control code in JavaScript; the ZK engine creates the control code. And again, ZUML, which is easy to understand and use, offers an intuitive way to create web applications.

ZK also demonstrates its flexibility in this example—ZK supports JavaScript, if necessary, and many convenient tools including Dojo, FCKeditor, CAPTCHA, and Google Maps.

CHAPTER 7

Linking the GUI to a Database

Now that you've finished creating the GUI pages, it is time to handle the database part. The original Java Pet Store 2.0 sample program uses a Java persistent API (EJB3) to persist the model object. In ZK Pet Shop, I will use the Hibernate persistent layer to do the same thing. The good news is that the persistence mechanisms of EJB3 and Hibernate are almost the same, so the only thing you'll have to do is replace the EJB3 entity manager with Hibernate's thread session facility to handle database transactions.

The first two sections of this chapter, "Preparing the Database Environment" and "JDBC and Connection Pool," illustrate how to build the database environment manually. If you are familiar with these topics, you can skip to "Making ZK Work with Hibernate."

Preparing the Database Environment

Before diving into the mechanism of the persistent layer, you have to prepare the database environment, including installing the database and creating the required tables for ZK Pet Shop.

Downloading HSQL Database

In ZK Pet Shop, the HSQL Database Engine (HSQLDB) is adopted, since it is small, fast, and supports tables stored in memory or on a disk drive. HSQLDB can be downloaded from its project web site at the following URL: http://sourceforge.net/projects/hsqldb/.

The installation of HSQLDB is easy, you simply unzip the archive file, and copy hsqldb\lib\hsqldb.jar to the following directory:
$Eclipse_HOME\workspace\zkPetShop\WebContent\WEB-INF\lib.

Creating the ZK Pet Shop Tables

Once you have downloaded and installed HSQLDB, the next step is to create a database and the required tables to go with it. Follow these steps to open a command line program and launch the database management client:

1. Click Start ➤ Run.

2. Type **cmd** in the Open field, and click OK.

3. A black prompt window will open; click in the black window.

4. Type **cd $Eclipse_HOME\workspace\zkPetShop\WebContent\WEB-INF\lib** at the command line.

5. Execute the following command to activate the database management client:

```
java -cp hsqldb.jar org.hsqldb.util.DatabaseManager
```

Note ➡ Recall that $Eclipse_HOME represents the home directory of this book's Eclipse installation, which is explained in Chapter 4.

If the program is activated successfully, the Connect dialog box shown in Figure 7-1 will open.

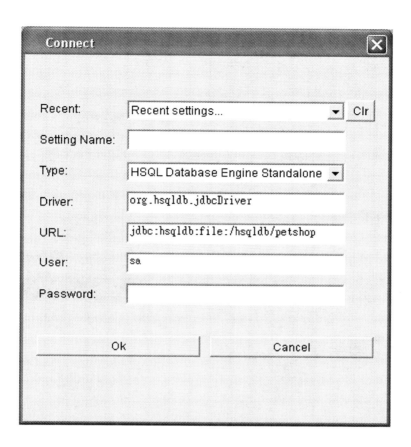

Figure 7-1. The pop-up connection dialog box of HSQLDB

Follow these steps to create the required tables for ZK Pet Shop:

1. Use the configuration information in Table 7-1 to fill in the required attributes in the Connect dialog box, and then click the OK button.

Table 7-1. Configuration of HSQLBD

Field	Function	Attribute
Type	Type of HSQLDB	HSQL database engine standalone
Driver	Driver	org.hsqldb.jdbcDriver
URL	Location of database	jdbc:hsqldb:file:/hsqldb/petshop
User	Authentication	sa
Password	Authentication	--

2. Select File ➤ Open Script in the HSQL Database Manager, as shown in Figure 7-2.

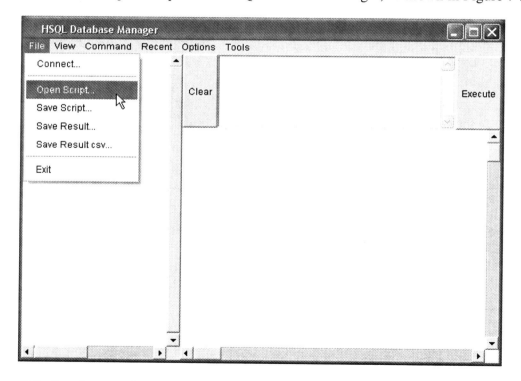

Figure 7-2. Opening a script in the HSQLDB Database Manager

3. Load the SQL script file petshop.sql from the following directory:

$Eclipse_HOME\workspace\zkPetShop\WebConent\WEB-INF\classes

4. Click the Execute button.

5. If this SQL script is executed successfully, you should see the message shown in Figure 7-3.

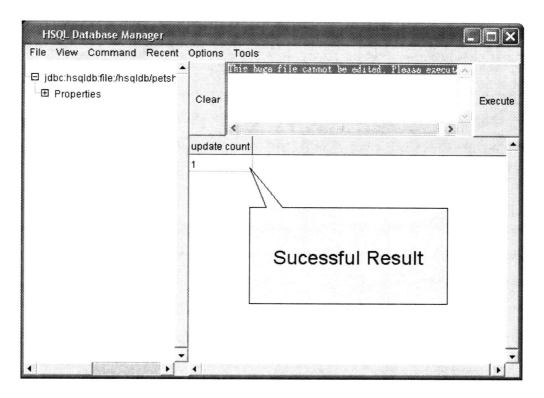

Figure 7-3. The HSQL Database Manager execution message

6. Select File ➤ Exit.

JDBC and Connection Pool

In order to access the database, we need to use Java Database Connectivity (JDBC), which is an API for the Java programming language that defines how a client may access a database and provides methods for querying and updating data in a database. In HSQLDB, the JDBC driver is included in the hsql.jar file.

Though using JDBC to establish database connection directly is convenient, some drawbacks exist, including longer response times for establishing database connections and less efficient database management. Thus, in this application, I prefer to use connection pool that has prepared a database connection in advance to shorten the response times and so that database connections can be recycled; this feature is supported by Tomcat 5.5.

Note ➡ For more information about JDBC, see http://java.sun.com/javase/technologies/database/, and for more on connection pools, http://en.wikipedia.org/wiki/Connection_pool.

Establishing a connection pool in Tomcat 5.5 is easy with the help of the Java Naming Directory Interface (JNDI), which enables applications to access naming and directory services. To use JNDI in Tomcat 5.5 requires the following steps:

1. Create a file called context.xml in the zkPetShop/WebContent/META-INF/ directory.

2. Edit context.xml to add the following database configuration information, as shown in Listing 7-1:

    •   Resource name: Name of resource

    •   username: User authentication for establishing database connection

    •   password: Password authentication for establishing database connection

    •   auth: Indicates who is responsible for authentication

    •   url: URL to look up the database resource

    •   driverClassName: Driver to establish database connection

    •   type: Type of resource

Listing 7-1. Adding Database Configuration to context.xml

```
<context>
<!-- The connection pool will be bound into JNDI with the name ➡
"java:comp/env/jdbc/hsql"-->
<Resource name="jdbc/hsql"
username="sa" password=""
url="jdbc:hsqldb:file:/hsqldb/petshop"
auth="Container" defaultAutoCommit="false"
driverClassName="org.hsqldb.jdbcDriver" maxActive="20"
timeBetweenEvictionRunsMillis="60000"
type="javax.sql.DataSource"/>
</context>
```

3. Open web.xml in the zkPetShop/WebContent/WEB-INF/ directory for editing.

4. In web.xml, add the resource configurations between </context> tags, as shown in Listing 7-2.

Listing 7-2. Adding Resource Configurations to web.xml

```
<context>
...................................
<resource-ref>
<res-ref-name>jdbc/hsql</res-ref-name>
<res-type>javax.sql.DataSource</res-type>
<res-auth>Container</res-auth>
</resource-ref>
</context>
```

Notice that all of the attributes mentioned in the preceding web.xml file must follow the configurations in context.xml. Table 7-2 lists the mapping between the attributes.

Table 7-2. Attribute Mapping Between web.xml and context.xml

<resource-ref> in web.xml	<context/> in Context.xml
res-ref-name	Resource name
res-type	type
res-auth	auth

Making ZK Work with Hibernate

Hibernate is an object-relational mapping (ORM) solution for the Java language. The main feature of Hibernate is that it simplifies the job of accessing a database, which usually requires tedious code in the form of select, add, delete and update Structured Query Language (SQL) statements. For instance, you could use the select SQL statement in Listing 7-3 to get information about a pet from the Item table using its ItemID. To code this with SQL, you have to write the SQL statement, manage the database connection, and duplicate data from ResultSet to the Item object all by yourself.

Listing 7-3. Hulking Code Created Using SQL Statements Without ORM

```
public Item getItem(Long itemID){
    Context initContext = new InitialContext();
    Context envContext = (Context) initContext.lookup("java:/comp/env");
    DataSource ds = (DataSource) envContext.lookup("jdbc/hsql ");
    Connection conn = ds.getConnection();
    Statement stmt = con.createStatement();

ResultSet rs = stmt.executeQuery("select * from Item ➡
where ItemID = '" + itemID +"'");
    rs.next();
    Item result.ITEMID = rs.getInt(1);
    result.PRODUCTID = rs.getString(2);
    result.NAME = rs.getString(3);
    resulf.IMAGEURL = rs.getString(4);
    result.DESCRIPTION = rs.getString(5);
    result.IMAGETHUMBURL = rs.getString(6);
    result.PRICE = rs.getDecimal(7);
    ...............................
    rs.close();
    stmt.close(0;
    conn.close(0;
}
```

Are you tired of this tedious work? Let's take a look at code that performs the same query with Hibernate in Listing 7-4.

Listing 7-4. Using Hibernate to Query a Database

```
public Item getItem(Long itemID){
    Item result = (Item) HibernateUtil.currentSession() ➦
.load(Item.class, itemID);
    return result;
}
```

Wow! Look how much thinner the code shown in Listing 7-4 is. If you simply invoke the load() method, Hibernate does all the tedious work of creating the SQL statement, including duplicating data from the resultset to an Item object, and managing the database connection. This is the whole idea of ORM—to copy data from table to an object so that you can deal with Java object directly without handling the query results from the database.

Another characteristic of Hibernate is persistence, which keeps object data consistent with table data to help you store data from an object to a table. In the following section, you will learn all the prerequisites of using Hibernate.

Prerequisites of Using Hibernate

Only a few steps are required to make Hibernate work for you. The first step is to create a Java class corresponding to the table in the database. Then, edit the Hibernate configuration file according to your requirements. The last step is to set up Hibernate mapping among the Java class and the tables in the database.

Creating the Java Class

First of all, you should create a Java class that defines the attributes of an object and attribute-related getter and setter methods. For example, take the Item class, which defines attributes of a pet in the ZK Pet Shop; attributes about a pet include the pet's name, description, price, and the URL of its photo. Listing 7-5 shows part of the Item class.

Listing 7-5. The Item.java Class (Derived from the Java Pet Store Application)

```
public class Item implements java.io.Serializable {
   private Long itemID;
   private String productID;
   private String name;
   private String description;
   private String imageURL;

   ................................................................
   public Long getItemID() {
      return itemID;
   }
   public String getProductID() {
      return productID;
   }
   public void setItemID(Long itemID) {
      this.itemID = itemID;
   }
   public void setProductID(String productID) {
      this.productID = productID;
   }
}
```

Editing the Hibernate Configuration File

The second step is to edit the required configurations in hibernate.cfg.xml, which must be placed at the root directory of context classpath of the web application (for example, WEB-INF/classes). Listing 7-6 shows the configuration file of ZK Pet Shop, including the database connection via JNDI, database configuration, and mapping of those classes that require persistence.

Listing 7-6. Editing the hibernate.cfg.xml File

```
<?xml version='1.0' encoding='utf-8'?>
<!DOCTYPE hibernate-configuration PUBLIC" ➥
//-Hibernate/Hibernate Configuration DTD 3.0//EN" ➥
"http://hibernate.sourceforge.net/hibernate-configuration-3.0.dtd">

<hibernate-configuration>
    <session-factory>
```

```
        <!-- connnect via JNDI -->
    <property name="hibernate.connection.datasource">
java:comp/env/jdbc/hsql
</property>
        <!-- SQL dialect -->
        <propertyname="dialect">
    org.hibernate.dialect.HSQLDialect
        </property>
        <!-- Patch the HSQL error for batching -->
        <property name="hibernate.jdbc.batch_size">0</property>
        <!-- Enable Hibernate's automatic session context management -->
        <property name="current_session_context_class">thread</property>
        <!-- Disable the second-level cache  -->
        <property name="cache.provider_class">
    org.hibernate.cache.NoCacheProvider
</property>
        <!-- Echo all executed SQL to stdout -->
        <property name="show_sql">true</property>
        <!-- Drop and re-create the database schema on startup -->
        <property name="hbm2ddl.auto">false</property>
    <!-- Mapping persistence classes -->
    <mapping class="org.zkforge.petshop.model.Address"/>
    <mapping class="org.zkforge.petshop.model.Category"/>
    <mapping class="org.zkforge.petshop.model.Item"/>
    <mapping class="org.zkforge.petshop.model.Product"/>
    <mapping class="org.zkforge.petshop.model.SellerContactInfo"/>
    <mapping class="org.zkforge.petshop.model.Tag"/>
    <mapping class="org.zkforge.petshop.model.ZipLocation"/>
    </session-factory>
</hibernate-configuration>
```

Mapping Object Resources

In addition to creating Java classes, you need to tell Hibernate about the relationships among Java classes and tables in the database to accomplish the ORM.

There are two ways to tell Hibernate how to map Java classes to tables. One is to create a mapping file, and the other is to use Java annotation. The next sections will explore both of them, so that we can choose the best solution for the ZK Pet Shop.

Using a Mapping File

Let's use the Item class as an example for creating a mapping file for ORM. First of all, create an Item.hbm.xml file in the same directory as your Java source file using the configuration in Listing 7-7; the following components and attributes are added to the file:

- class: Specifies the Java class
  - name: Name of Java class
  - table: Name of table
- id: Specifies the primary key of the table
  - name: Name of the attribute in the Java class
  - column: Name of a column in the table
- property: Specifies information of other, related attributes
  - name: Name of the attributes of the Java class
  - type: The attribute's data type
  - column: The name of the attribute's column in the table

Note ➡ The prefix of the XXX.hbm.xml file must be the name of Java class (XXX.java).

Listing 7-7. Item.hbm.xml

```
<hibernate-mapping>
 <class name="org.zkforge.petshop.model.Item" table="Item">
  <id name="id" column="id">
   <generator class="native"/>
  </id>
  <property name="itemID" type="string" column="itemID"/>
  <property name="productID" type="string" column="productID"/>
 </class>
</hibernate-mapping>
```

Using Java Annotations

As an alternative to creating external configuration files, Java 5.0 introduces the idea of annotation for adding related descriptions inside a Java class. Listing 7-8 demonstrates the use of annotation in our example Item class. The @Entity annotation declares the class to be persistent; in other words, data will be dumped from memory into the database. The @Id annotation indicates the property that is the unique identifier for this class. More modifiers of annotation will be introduced in the section called "The ZK Pet Shop Data Model with Annotations."

Listing 7-8. Using Java Annotation

```
@Entity
@Table(name="Item")
public class Item implements java.io.Serializable {
    private Long itemID;
    private String productID;
    ...............................................................
@Id
@Column(name="code", length=5)
    public Long getItemID() {
        return itemID;
    }
}
```

As you can see, Java annotations provide a more intuitive way of mapping Java classes and tables in the database, since you can modify related information in the Java class directly without modifying an external file. Besides, annotations are easier to use and don't require much configuration. Therefore, let's adopt Java annotations for Hibernate mapping tasks in the ZK Pet Shop application.

Advanced Features of Hibernate

In this section, I will introduce you two frequently encountered problems of database management on the Internet and how Hibernate deals with these problems.

Units of Work

Data consistency among related data is important in database management, especially in an Internet environment, where a business transaction might be interrupted by unknown Internet factors before modifying all related data.

To avoid inconsistency difficulties, the idea of "all or nothing" is introduced into database management. This means that the SQL operations that alter related data in the database should be committed only when a particular group of database access operations is accomplished without interruption or errors; otherwise, the series of access operations should be regarded as invalid. To realize this idea, a unit of work keeps track of all SQL data manipulating language (DML) operations (update, insert, and delete) during a business transaction.

A Hibernate session is usually regarded as one unit of work. To begin a unit of work, you open a session, and to end a unit of work, you close a session.

Note ➡ For more information about units of work in Hibernate, you can visit www.hibernate.org/42.html#A2.

Keeping a Session Open

A common use for a session in a typical web application is the rendering of the view. You might have to access several different persistent objects to show a view. You want to access these persistent objects in a single Hibernate session so that the data consistency is guaranteed, so keep the session open until the view has been completely rendered.

You should use a request interceptor to open the session right after the request is received by the server. Then commit database transactions, and close the session right before the response is sent to the client. To make the use of the interceptor possible, ZK provides a listener (OpenSessionInViewListener) that implements both the ExecutionInit interface, which begins a session when an execution is created, and the ExecutionCleanup interface, which closes the session when this execution is complete and ready to be destroyed.

Note ➡ When the ZK loader and update engine create a new execution, the ZK loader will invoke the init() method of the org.zkoss.zk.ui.util.ExecutionInit interface, so that you can plug in the application-specific code to initialize an execution. Conversely, ZK loader invokes the cleanup() method of the org.zkoss.zk.ui.util.ExecutionCleanup interface when this execution is complete.

Configuring ZK for Use with Sessions

To adopt open session functionalities, the configurations shown in Listing 7-9 are required; edit zk.xml in the $Eclipse_HOME\workspace\zkPetShop\WebContent\WEB-INF directory as shown in the listing.

Listing 7-9. Configuring zk.xml to Use Sessions

```
<!-- Configure the Hibernate SessionFactory Lifecycle.-->
<listener>
<description>Hibernate SessionFactory Lifecycle</description>
<listener-class>
org.zkoss.zkplus.hibernate.HibernateSessionFactoryListener
</listener-class>
</listener>
<!-- Configure the Hibernate "Open Session In View" Session Lifecycle -->
<listener>
<description>Hibernate "Open Session In View" Session Lifecycle ➡
</description>
<listener-class>
org.zkoss.zkplus.hibernate.OpenSessionInViewListener
</listener-class>
</listener>
<!-- Hibernate thread session context handler -->
<listener>
<description>Hibernate thread session context handler</description>
<listener-class>
org.zkoss.zkplus.hibernate.HibernateSessionContextListener
</listener-class>
</listener>
```

Note ➡ For more information about configuring Hibernate to use sessions, please use the following URL: http://www.zkoss.org/smalltalks/hibernatezk/hibernatezk.dsp.

The ZK Pet Shop Data Model with Annotations

The data model of the ZK Pet Shop application is based on the data model of Java Pet Store 2.0. Figure 7-4 graphs the relationship among tables in the ZK Pet Shop.

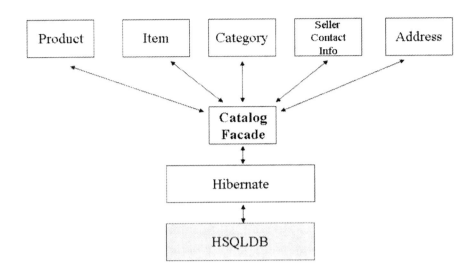

Figure 7-4. The data model of the ZK Pet Shop application

Table 7-3 lists the functions of each table included in this data model.

Table 7-3. Functions of Tables in the ZK Pet Shop's Data Model

Table	Function
ADDRESS	Stores the address of the seller
CATEGORY	Stores the pet's category
ITEM	Stores the descriptions and attributes of a pet
PRODUCT	Stores the subtype of a pet's category, for example, "hairy cat"
SELLERCONTACTINFO	Stores the seller's contact information

Table Annotations

I am going to introduce you the ORM annotations used to map Java classes and tables in the database. Two steps are required to declare a class as an entity bean (an object stored in persistent storage or a database). The first step is to add the @Entity annotation before the declaration of the class. Next, you should tell Hibernate which table should be mapped with this Java class; specify a database table to the entity bean with the @Table annotation.

Listing 7-10 shows an example using the Item class.

Listing 7-10. Example of @Entity and @Table

```
@Entity
@Table(name=Item)
public class Item implements java.io.Serializable {
……………………………
}
```

Property Annotations

For data persistence, getter and setter methods of attributes defined in a Java class should be correlated with their corresponding columns in the database tables. Use the @Column annotation to specify the SQL column name associated with a class. Listing 7-11 shows the usage of the @Column annotation; you should put an @Column annotation above the declaration of the getter method of the specified attribute.

Listing 7-11. Example of @Column

```
@Column(name="ItemID")    //could be omitted
public Long getItemID() {
      return itemID;
   }
public void setItemID(String itemid){
      this.itemid = itemid;
}
@Column (name="ProductID") //could be omitted
public String getProductID() {
      return productID;
   }
public void setProductID(String productid){
    this.productid = productid
}
```

Note ➡ If the column name and property name of the class are the same, the @Column annotation can be omitted.

Primary Key Annotations

The @Id annotation is used to specify the primary key of a Java class. In our example Item class, you need to put the @Id annotation above the getItemID() method, which is a getter method of primary key ItemID. It is shown in listing 7-12.

Listing 7-12. Primary Key Annotation

```
@Id
public Long getItemID() {
   return itemID;
}
```

In addition, automatically generating the primary key decreases the number of database access queries needed to retrieve tables' primary keys. Both the @TableGenerator and @GeneratedValue annotations are used to automatically generate primary keys. These annotations should be placed above the @Id annotation. Listing 7-13 demonstrates their use.

Listing 7-13. Annotations for Automatically Generating Primary Keys

```
@TableGenerator(name="ITEM_ID_GEN",
      table="ID_GEN",
      pkColumnName="GEN_KEY",
      valueColumnName="GEN_VALUE",
      pkColumnValue="ITEM_ID",
      allocationSize=1)
@GeneratedValue(strategy=GenerationType.TABLE,generator="ITEM_ID_GEN")
@Id
public Long getItemID() {
return itemID;
}
```

This section has introduced some of the basic annotations used in the data model of the ZK Pet Shop application. Table 7-4 lists all of the annotations used in this application, so you can look up any that haven't been covered in detail in this chapter.

Table 7-4. Annotations Used in ZK Pet Shop

Annotations	Functions
@Entity	Annotates the specified class as an entity bean
@Table	Specifies the database table for an entity bean. The default table name is the class name.
@Id	Marks a field as a primary key
@Column	Specifies the SQL column name of this field
@Table Generator	Used with @Id to specify an automatic key generator when new objects are created
@GeneratedValue	Used with @Id to specify an automatic key generator when new objects are created
@NamedQueries	Creates a list of all the named queries used in a class
@NamedQuery	Specifies a named query in the Java persistence query language, which is a static query expressed in metadata
@Transient	Marks the data in the field as data that should not be persisted (not be saved)
@OneToOne	Marks a field as belonging to a one-to-one (dependent linked) relationship
@ManyToMany	Marks a field as belonging to a many-to-one (linked) relationship

Implementing the Façade Class of the ZK Pet Shop

In this chapter's previous sections, I have introduced you the database environment of the ZK Pet Shop application and explained how to use Hibernate with ZK. Now, we'll undertake the last mile of the ZK Pet Shop—we'll create the CatalogFacade class, which glues the GUI parts and the database together.

The CatalogFacade Class

The CatalogFacade class is built based on a façade pattern. The CatalogFacade class acts as a bridge between the controller and data model and is responsible for accessing data from the database using Hibernate. All database-related control code is included in this class for easier maintenance in the future and to maintain a clear demarcation between the controller and data model. Table 7-5 lists the most often used methods in CatalogFacade and their functions.

Note ➡ For more information about Façade pattern, please visit this URL:
http://en.wikipedia.org/wiki/Fa%C3%A7ade_pattern.

Table 7-5. Frequently Used Methods in CatalogFacade

Method	Function
getCategories()	Get categories of pets
getProducts()	Get products of a certain category
getItems()	Get items by product ID
addItem(Item)	Save both the pet's and seller's information
getItemsByCategoryByRadiusVLH()	Get those items (pets) that belong a certain category and are located in a defined range

Implementing the CatalogFacade Class with Hibernate

In this section, I will show you how to implement the frequently used methods in Table 7-5 using Hibernate. They are separated into two groups: one using the SELECT statement and the other, the INSERT statement. The next two sections will show you the convenience of accessing database through Hibernate.

SELECT Statement

The first example using a SELECT statement is getCategories(), shown in Listing 7-14. The getCategories() method gets all kinds of pet categories from the Category table.

Listing 7-14. getCategories()

```
public List<Category> getCategories(){
  List<Category> categories = HibernateUtil.currentSession() ➡
.createQuery("FROM Category").list();
  return categories;
}
```

In Listing 7-15, the getProducts() method gets all kinds of pet products from the Product table and stores the query result into a products data collection.

Listing 7-15. getProducts()

```
public List<Product> getProducts(){
    List<Product> products = HibernateUtil.currentSession() ➡
    .createQuery("FROM Product").list();
    return products;
  }
```

In Listing 7-16, the getItems() method finds all pet data in the Item table corresponding to the specified product ID.

Listing 7-16. getItems()

```
public List<Item> getItems(String prodID){
    List<Item> items = HibernateUtil.currentSession() ➥
.createQuery("FROM Item i WHERE i.productID LIKE : ➥
productID AND i.disabled = 0").setParameter("productID" ➥
,prodID).list();
    return items;
}
```

The last example is the getItemsByCategoryByRadiusVLH() method, which finds all pet data that meets the specified criteria, including category ID, longitude, and latitude data.

Listing 7-17. getItemsByCategoryByRadiusVLH()

```
public List<Item> getItemsByCategoryByRadiusVLH(String catID, int start,
  int chunkSize,double fromLat,double toLat,double fromLong,
    double toLong){
    List<Item> items = HibernateUtil.currentSession() ➥
    .createQuery("SELECT i FROM Item i, Product p WHERE " ➥
    + "i.productID=p.productID AND p.categoryID = :catID " ➥
    + "AND((i.address.latitude BETWEEN :fromLat AND :toLat) ➥
AND " + "(i.address.longitude BETWEEN :fromLong AND :toLong )) ➥
AND i.disabled = 0" + " ORDER BY i.name") ➥
.setParameter("catID",catID) .setParameter("fromLat",fromLat) ➥
.setParameter("toLat",toLat) .setParameter("fromLong",fromLong) ➥
.setParameter("toLong",toLong).setFirstResult(start) ➥
.setMaxResults(chunkSize).list();
    return items;
  }
```

INSERT Statement

Listing 7-18 shows an example of an INSERT statement using Hibernate. The Session.persist() method is invoked to save data into a database table after a transaction is committed.

Listing 7-18. addItem()

```
public Long addItem(Item item){
    Session session = HibernateUtil.currentSession();
    for(Tag tag : item.getTags()) {
```

```
      tag.incrementRefCount();
      tag.getItems().add(item);
   }
   session.persist(item);
   return item.getItemID();
}
```

User's Activities and the Behind-the-Scene Mechanism

In this section, I will explain the behind-the-scene mechanism of the ZK Pet Shop application activated by users' activities. The mechanism illustrates the interactivity among the viewer, controller, and data model. I've choose four requirements of ZK Pet Shop for explanation.

The User Submits a Pet for Sale

After entering all required data for a pet, the user will click the Submit button, and the SellerWindow class will collect data from the UI components and invoke the addItem() method of the CatalogFacade class to save the pet's data into the database. Here's a breakdown of what happens behind the scenes as a result of the user's activity:

- *User's activity*: The user clicks the Submit button.
- *Behind the scenes*: The pet and seller data is saved into the database.
    1. SellerWindow collects data from the UI components and sends a request for saving the pet's information to CatalogFacade.
    2. CatalogFacade.addItem() saves all required data to the database via Hibernate and returns a new ItemId.
    3. SellerWindow acquires the ItemId and puts it into the UI component.
- *Result*: A successful submission message

The diagram in Figure 7-5 illustrates this sequence of events.

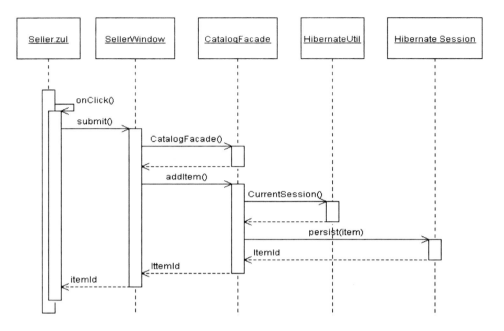

Figure 7-5. Submitting a pet's information

The User Visits catalog.zul for the First Time

When the user visits catalog.zul for the first time, a lot of data is required to present the UI components, which include pet categories, products, and information; the location of image files; and so on. Here's what happens behind the scenes when a user first visits ZK Pet Shop:

- *User's activity*: The user requests the catalog.zul URL.
- *Behind the scenes*: Fetch the pet information from the database.
    1. The CatalogWindow class sends a request for data to the CatalogFacade class.

    2. CatalogFacade gets all the required data from the database using Hibernate.

    3. CatalogWindow supplies the data to the UI components.
- *Result*: The pets' categories, products, photos, and so forth are shown in the UI.

Figure 7-6 illustrates the communication between the controller and the CatalogFacade class with more details.

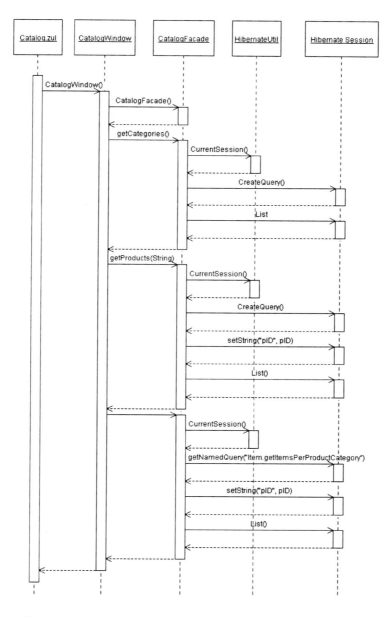

Figure 7-6. Requesting catalog.zul for the first time

Browse Pets of a Certain Product Type

When the user clicks any type of pet, the photos in both the middle pane and the gallery will be refreshed. Behind the scenes, the controller will send a request for the pet information for the product type chosen by the user:

- *User's activity*: The user clicks any pet product type on the menu bar.
- *Behind the scenes*: Get pet information for the selected pet product type.

   1. CatalogWindow sends a request for data of the selected pet product type to CatalogFacade.

   2. CatalogFacade gets all required data from the database through Hibernate.

   3. CatalogWindow displays the data in the UI components.

- *Result*: The pets' photos and descriptions are refreshed.

   In Figure 7-7, a sequence diagram shows what happens when the user clicks the hyperlink for a pet product type.

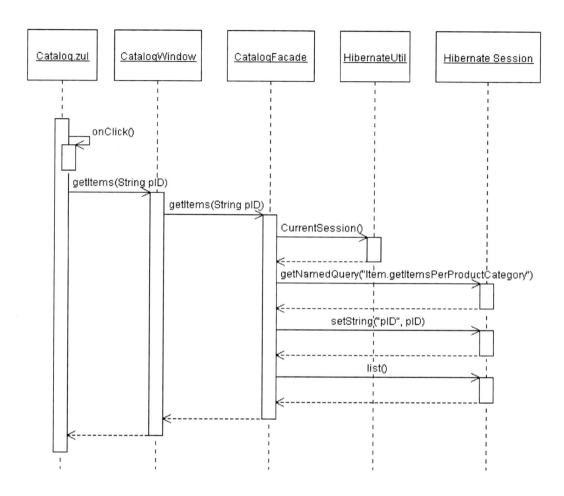

Figure 7-7. Browsing a selected type of pet product

Searching for a Pet's Location with Google Maps

When the user clicks the Search button to send a query for a pet's location, the controller interprets this query, gets the required data from the database, and shows the result on the UI components. Behind the scenes, this is what happens:

- *User's activity*: The user clicks the Search button.
- *Behind the scenes*: Get all pets qualify the specified criteria by the user.
    1. The MapWindow class sends the required information to the CatalogFacade class.
    2. CatalogFacade gets the required data, based on the conditions defined by the user, from the database using Hibernate.
    3. MapWindow acquires the necessary data and displays it in the UI components.
- *Result*: The pets' location is shown using Google Maps, and a table of pets' information is displayed.

Figure 7-8 illustrates the behind-the-scenes mechanism that's initiated when the user clicks the Search button after entering all required data to search for a pet's location.

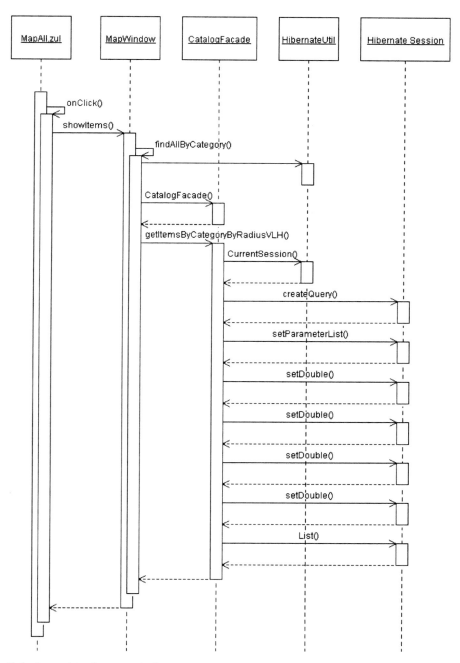

Figure 7-8. Searchig for a pet's location

Summary

In this chapter, I have introduced you to setting up a database environment for ZK Pet Shop and some mechanisms that drive Hibernate.

Moreover, I've illustrated how to establish the last link between the controllers and the data model for the ZK Pet Shop, that is, how to retrieve data from and save it to the database. Now that you have all the controller and model code in place, you can see that ZK Pet Shop is a good model of the MVC design pattern, since each of these three parts is clearly demarcated.

Is this the end of ZK Pet Shop? Not yet! In the final chapter, I will introduce you the data binding mechanism that will further simply the code required to drive your controllers.

CHAPTER 8

Binding Data Automatically

In previous chapters, ZK Pet Shop demonstrated the power of ZK by allowing you to separate a web application into its model, view, and controller parts without much effort. Now, we are going to make moving data between ZK components and the data model smoother, especially the plumbing code—loading data from the model to the ZK components and saving data from ZK components to the data model.

Getting Rid of The Plumbing Code

As an example, let's take a look at a code snippet extracted from the SellerWindow class that is responsible for collecting the seller's name and address information from each of the ZK components that stores the data. Listing 8-1 uses several getFellow() and getValue() methods to obtain data from UI components. Retrieving information in this way is tedious but indispensable, but ZK offers a way to help simplify this nightmare of repetitive plumbing code using the ZUML Annotations and ZK AnnotateDataBinder classes.

Listing 8-1. Example of Plumbing Code from SellerWindow

```
{
//contact
    String firstName = ((Textbox)getFellow("firstName")).getValue();
    String lastName = ((Textbox)getFellow("lastName")).getValue();
    String email = ((Textbox)getFellow("email")).getValue();
    //Address
    String street1 = ((Textbox)getFellow("street")).getValue();
    String city = ((Textbox)getFellow("city")).getValue();
    String state = ((Textbox)getFellow("state")).getValue();
    String zip = ((Textbox)getFellow("zipCode")).getValue();
}
```

Using the ZUML Annotations Class

The ZUML Annotations class is inspired by Java 5 annotations. ZUML annotations provide metadata about a component that is examined by an external tool, called a data binding manager, at runtime for further processing. For example, a data binding manager might examine annotations to understand the relationship between a ZK component's attributes and the data model to move data from the data model to the ZK components; the annotations tell the data binding manager the source and destination of the data.

Formatting Data Binding Annotations

You need to declare data binding annotations before declaring the ZK components that they bind. Listing 8-2 shows the format of ZK data binding annotation: basically, begin with a short prefix of the Annotation namespace (a), followed by a colon (:) and the data binding annotation (bind).

Listing 8-2. Format of Data Binding Annotations

```
<a:bind attribX="attribY;[tag:expression]"/>
<ComponentX/>
```

Here are the details that compose the data binding annotation:

- a: The short prefix of the XML namespace of Annotation
- bind: The data binding annotation
- attribX: An attribute of ComponentX
- attribY: An attribute in the data model that corresponds to attribX
- tag: Specifies which tag is used (See the next section for more information.)
- expression: Used along with tag to provide more details
- ComponentX: A component that contains the attribute specified in attribX

Listing 8-3 provides an example in which the data binding manager will automatically put the seller.firstName and seller.lastName label components into listcell components.

Listing 8-3. Mapping listcell to a Seller's Attributes

```
<?init class="org.zkoss.zkplus.databind.AnnotateDataBinderInit" ?>
<window xmlns:a="http://www.zkoss.org/2005/zk/annotation">
<zscript src = "seller.zs">
   Seller seller = new Seller();
</zscript>
  <listbox rows="4">
    <listitem>
    <a:bind label="seller.firstName"/>
    <listcell/>
    <a:bind label="seller.lastName"/>
    <listcell/>
    </listitem>
  </listbox>
</window>
```

The Seller class used in the previous example is defined in Listing 8-4.

Listing 8-4. The Seller Class Defined in seller.zs

```
public class Seller {
   private String firstName="";
   private String lastName="";

   //getter and setters
   public void setFirstName(String firstName) {
      this.firstName = firstName;
   }
   public String getFirstName() {
      return this.firstName;
   }
   public void setLastName(String lastName) {
      this.lastName = lastName;
   }
   public String getLastName() {
      return this.lastName;
   }
}
```

Using Data Binding with the ZK Annotations Class

Follow these steps to use a data binding manager in your ZK application:

1. Declare the ZK Annotation namespace using xmlns with a short prefix, for example, a:

```
<window xmlns:a="http://www.zkoss.org/2005/zk/annotation">
```

Note ➡ The xmlns element is used to declare the XML namespace adopted in the .zul page .

---

2. Initialize the AnnotateDataBinderInit class in the page-creation phase:

```
<?init class="org.zkoss.zkplus.databind.AnnotateDataBinderInit"?>
```

This initiator class will do following jobs:

   a. Create a new AnnotateDataBinder instance.

   b. Set the AnnotateDataBinder instance as a variable, binder, in the Page.

   c. Invoke the binder.loadAll() method to initiate all UI components from the associated data model.

3. Define the required annotations before declaring each ZK component. In the following example, the value attribute of the textbox component is mapped to the firstName attribute of the seller instance:

```
<a:bind value = "seller.firstName"/>
<textbox/>
```

4. You must specify events using an event tag within the annotation that invokes the data binding manager, or nothing will happen. In the following example, the save-when event tag is used to tell the data binding manager when to save data from UI components into the data model:

```
<a:bind value = "seller.firstName;save-when:self.onChange"/>
<textbox/>
```

The data binding manager will save value of textbox component into the firstName attribute of a seller instance when its value is changed. Table 8-1 lists the two most frequently used tags of the AnnotateDataBinder class: load-when and save-when.

Table 8-1. The load-when and save-when Tags for the AnnotateDataBinder Class

Tag Name	Tag Function	Attribute	Multiple Definitions Allowed
load-when	Specify events that invoke the data binding manager to load data from the data model to ZK components	Events or none	Yes
save-when	Specify events that invoke the data binding manager to save data from the ZK components to the data model	Events or none	No

The load-when Tag

With the load-when tag, you can specify the events that will trigger the data binding manager to load the attribute of the component from the data model to the ZK component. Multiple definitions are allowed and, if used, are called one by one. For example, the value attribute of fullName will load the value attribute from the person.fullName component when the firstName or lastName text box's onChange event is fired:

```
<a:bind value="person.firstName"/>
<textbox id="firstname"/>
<a:bind value="person.lastName"/>
<textbox id="lastname"/>
<a:bind value="person.fullName;load-when:firstname.onChange; ➡
load-when:lastname.onChange"/>
<label id="fullname"/>
```

The save-when Tag

You can specify the event that will trigger the data-binding manager to save the attribute of the component into the data model by using the save-when tag. For example, the value attribute of the firstName text box will be saved into the firstName attribute of person instance when the textbox itself fires its onChange event:

```
<a:bind value="person.firstName; save-when:self.onChange"/>
<textbox id="firstName"/>
```

Multiple definitions are *not* allowed; if you define more than one, the last one defined will override any previous ones.

If you don't specify any event tag within the annotation, the default events that are used depend on the natural characteristics of the component's attribute. For example, the default setting of a label's save-when tag is none, and for the text box component, it's self.onChange. Thus, the following example works the same as the previous one:

```
<a:bind value="person.firstName"/>
<textbox id="firstName"/>
```

However, you might want to neither specify the save-when tag nor use the default events. In that case, you can specify the none keyword:

```
<a:bind value="person.firstName; save-when:none;"/>
<textbox id="firstName"/>
```

or simply leave the tag empty, as shown in the following example:

```
<a:bind value="person.firstName; save-when: ;"/>
<textbox id="firstName"/>
```

Adding Data Binding to the ZK Pet Shop GUI

Now that you know how data binding works within ZK, I would like to illustrate data binding by showing you how to apply it to the ZK Pet Shop. Do you remember that we have to get information about the pet and the seller after the user's publication submission? Our first mission is getting the seller's information, including the seller's first name, last name, and e-mail address. Listing 8-4 illustrates getting data in the traditional way, which includes a lot of tedious plumbing code.

Listing 8-4. SellerWindow.java Without Data Binding

```
//contact
String firstName = ((Textbox)getFellow("firstName")).getValue();
String lastName = ((Textbox)getFellow("lastName")).getValue();
String email = ((Textbox)getFellow("email")).getValue();
......................................
SellerContactInfo contactInfo = new SellerContactInfo(firstName, ➥
lastName, email);
Item item = new Item(productId,petName,description,pictureURL, ➥
thumbURL,price,addr,contactInfo,0,0);
```

Believe it or not, using data binding allows you to remove all of the code in Listing 8-4 from the SellerWindow class, since its mission would be automatically accomplished by data binding.

Using Data Binding in the ZK Pet Shop

Use the following steps to make your thin-code dreams come true:

1. Declare getter and setter methods of the data model.

2. Declare the ZUML annotations namespace.

3. Define the data binding annotations.

4. Specify events that invoke the data-binding manager.

Declaring Getter and Setter Methods of the Data Model

The first step is to declare an instance of the Item class in the SellerWindow class to store the pet's and seller's information (the SellerContactInfo class is included within the Item class). In addition to declaring the Item class instance, you need to define the getter and setter methods of the Item instance in order for the data binding manager to access it (see Listing 8-5).

Listing 8-5. Declare an Item instance in the SellerWindow class

```
public class SellerWindow extends Window {
  private Item __item;
public SellerWindow() {
    item = new Item();
  }
  public Item getItem() {
   return __item;
  }
  public void setItem(Item item) {
    item = item;
  }
}
```

Note ➡ You don't have to declare Listings 8-6 and 8-7, since they have been declared; they are listed for explanation purposes.

Inside the Item class, a pair of getter and setter method are defined for accessing an instance of the SellerContactInfo class within Item, as shown in Listing 8-6.

Listing 8-6. Getter and Setter Methods for the SellerContactInfo Instance within the Item Class (Derived from the Java Pet Store Application)

```
private SellerContactInfo contactInfo;
.....................................
  public SellerContactInfo getContactInfo() {
    return contactInfo;
  }
  public void setContactInfo(SellerContactInfo contactInfo) {
    this.contactInfo = contactInfo;
  }
```

Listing 8-7 shows the attributes and methods for accessing members of the SellerContactInfo class.

Listing 8-7. Members and Methods Defined in the SellerContactInfo Class (Derived from the Java Pet Store Application)

```java
public class SellerContactInfo implements java.io.Serializable {
  private String lastName;
  private String firstName;
  private String email;

public String getLastName() {
    return lastName;
  }
  public String getFirstName() {
    return firstName;
  }
  public String getEmail() {
    return email;
  }
  public void setEmail(String email) {
    this.email = email;
  }
  public void setLastName(String lastName) {
    this.lastName = lastName;
  }
  public void setFirstName(String firstName) {
    this.firstName = firstName;
  }
}
}
```

Declaring the ZUML Annotations Namespace

The second step is to declare an Annotations namespace and to invoke an AnnotateDataBinderInit class initiator (see Listing 8-8).

Listing 8-8. Page Namespace Declaration

```xml
<?xml version="1.0" encoding="UTF-8" ?>
<?init class="org.zkoss.zkplus.databind.AnnotateDataBinderInit" ?>
<window id="win" use="org.zkforge.petshop.controller.SellerWindow" ➥
xmlns=http://www.zkoss.org/2005/zul ➥
xmlns:xsi=http://www.w3.org/2001/XMLSchema-instance ➥
xmlns:a="http://www.zkoss.org/2005/zk/annotation" ➥
xsi:schemaLocation="http://www.zkoss.org/2005/zul ➥
http://www.zkoss.org/2005/zul/zul.xsd">
```

Defining the Data Binding Annotations

The third step is to declare data-binding annotations. Listing 8-9 shows the code for the page without using data binding.

Listing 8-9. seller.zul Before Adding Data Binding

```
<row>*First Name:<textbox id="firstName"/></row>
<row>*Last name: <textbox id="lastName"/></row>
<row>Seller Email: <textbox id="email"/></row>
```

Our mission is to get the user information that is stored in the textbox component. In order to use the data binding manager to get these attributes, you should define related annotations before declaring each of the textbox components. Listing 8-10 shows the page's code after adopting data binding annotations.

Listing 8-10. seller.zul with Data Binding Annotations Added

```
<row>*First Name:
   <a:bind value="win.item.contactInfo.firstName"/>
   <textbox id="firstName"/>
</row>
<row>*Last name:
   <a:bind value="win.item.contactInfo.lastName"/>
<textbox id="lastName"/>
</row>
<row>Seller Email:
   <a:bind value="win.item.contactInfo.email"/>
<textbox id="email"/>
</row>
```

Before each textbox component's declaration, there needs to be a corresponding annotation that tells the data binding manager how to map the textbox component to the Item instance, which is a member of the window component. The relationships can be illustrated with the mappings shown in Table 8-2.

Table 8-2. The Mappings of textbox Components and the contactInfo instance

Attribute of textbox	Attribute of an Instance of the ContactInfo class (within the Item instance)
firstName.value	win.item.contactInfo.firstName
lastName.value	win.item.contactInfo.lastName
email.value	win.item.contactInfo.email

The data binding manager gets attributes defined within an instance of the ContactInfo class by sequentially invoking the methods listed in Table 8-3,

Table 8-3 Getting Attributes of an Instance of the ContactInfo class

Getter Method	Return Object
win.getItem()	An instance of the Item class
item.getContactInfo()	An instance of the ContactInfo class
contactinfo.getXXX()	An attribute of the contactInfo instance corresponding to the getter method

The data-binding manager saves data into the data model by invoking the setter methods defined in the data model.

Specifying Events that Invoke the Data-Binding Manager

The fourth step is to declare events within the annotation to invoke the data-binding manager to save or load data between ZK components and the data model. In Listing 8-11, the data binding manager will save the value of textbox into the contactInfo instance once the value of textbox is modified.

Listing 8-11. Specify Events Within the Annotation in seller.zul

```
<row>*First Name:
   <a:bind value="win.item.contactInfo.firstName; ➡
save-when:self.onChange"/>
   <textbox id="firstName"/>
</row>
<row>*Last name:
   <a:bind value="win.item.contactInfo.lastName; ➡
save-when:self.onChange"/>
<textbox id="lastName"/>
</row>
<row>Seller Email:
   <a:bind value="win.item.contactInfo.email;save-when:self.onChange"/>
<textbox id="email"/>
</row>
```

Note ➡ In fact, you don't have to specify the events in Listing 8-11, since they have been included in the default event tags of the textbox component.

As this section shows, you must complete several steps to use data binding, but the outcome is lovely. The tedious plumbing code for getting and saving data is no longer required, since all required data has been stored by data-binding manager—you simply need to store the Item instance in the database, as shown in Listing 8-12.

Listing 8-12. The submit() Method of the SellerWindow Class

```
public void submit(){
  Long itemId = new CatalogFacade().addItem(_item);
}
```

Using Data Binding with Data Collections

The previous example demonstrates how to use data binding to avoid the job of getting data from ZK components and saving it in the data model with one-to-one mapping. Next, I am going to tell you how to apply data binding to data collections, like Array, List, Set, and

Map. One thing I should remind you is that only Grid and Listbox components can be mapped to data collections, since they are more often used to show a large amount of data.

This time, our target is a List that stores pet's categories in the seller.zul page where a Listbox is used for displaying these categories. The steps to use data binding on a collection are the same as in the previous section, so I've chosen only the following two steps for explanation:

- Declare getter and setter methods of the data model.

- Define the data binding annotations.

Declaring Getter and Setter Methods of the Data Model

As in the previous example, the first step is to prepare the data model to use data binding. In Listing 8-13, products is a data collection that stores all kinds of pets' categories, and product—an instance of the Product class—is used to store the category chosen by the user. The default value of product is the first category stored in products. Listing 8-13 also declares the required getter and setter methods.

Listing 8-13. The Products Data Model

```
public class SellerWindow extends Window {
 private List _products;
 private Product _product;

 public List getProducts() {
  products = new CatalogFacade().getProducts();
 _product = (Product) _products.get(0);
  return _products;
  }
 public Product getProduct() {
  return _product;
  }
 public void setProduct(Product product) {
  this.product = product;
  }
 }
```

Defining the Data Binding Annotations

Next, you need to define the collection's data binding annotations, and the following two steps are required to perform many-to-many mapping between ZK components and the data collection:

1. Specify the data collection in the model attribute of listbox.

2. Define a template of ZK components using the _var tag.

Specifying the Data Collection in the model Attribute of listbox

In the first annotation, in Listing 8-14, the model attribute of the listbox component indicates the data collection used in listbox—that is, win.products—is assigned as the data collection of listbox in this example. In addition, the selectedItem attribute of listbox indicates the category chosen by the user, which is stored in win.product.

Listing 8-14. Products Data-Binding Annotations

```
<row>Category:
<a:bind model="win.products" selectedItem="win.product"/>
<listbox id="products" mold="select" rows="1">
<listitem/>
</listbox>
</row>
```

Defining a Template of ZK Components Using the _var Tag

In Listing 8-14, only one listitem is declared, but there are several types of categories in the ZK Pet Shop—one listitem won't be enough. Don't worry about this problem, because the data binding manger will handle it by creating the required ZK components automatically. How does the data binding manager know to construct ZK components? The answer is by giving an example—that is, a template—to it in the ZUML page using a special _var tag to define a name of the incoming instance from the data collection (win.products) used for that template, as follows:

```
<a:bind _var="product" value="product" label="product.name"/>
<listitem/>
```

The data binding manager will create a number of listitem components according to the number of instances in win.products. For each of the listitem components, a product instance will be assigned as a value of listitem, and a label whose value is product.name will be automatically attached to this listitem.

Summary

In this chapter, I have showed you how to use data binding, a powerful tool provided by ZK to handle the job of moving data. With the help of data binding, tedious but indispensable code, such as code to load and save data, can be eliminated.

Data binding not only supports one-to-one mapping between a ZK component and the data model but also supports many-to-many mappings for data collections, in which ZK components are created automatically according a predefined template with annotations.

CPSIA information can be obtained at www.ICGtesting.com
Printed in the USA
LVOW111033300912

300896LV00006B/7/A